Assyria and the Paris Peace Conference

ABRAHAM .K. YOOSUF

Assyria and the
Paris Peace Conference

EDITED BY

Tomas Beth-Avdalla

FOREWORD BY

Sargon George Donabed, Ph.D.

nineveh press

Abraham K. Yoosuf: Assyria and the Paris Peace Conference
MARA Collected Texts 2
Published by Nineveh Press
© Nineveh Press 2017
© Tomas Beth-Avdalla 2017
Designed by Tomas Beth-Avdalla, TBA Form
Set in Adobe Garamond Pro 10/14
Printed by: Lulu, Raleigh, NC, USA 2017
ISBN 978-91-984100-6-8
www.ninevehpress.com

Published with support from the Santakki Foundation, www.santakki.org.

In memory of the Assyrians who, during and after the Assyrian genocide, selflessly gave their all for the sake of their community and heritage

❧ Acknowledgments

George Donabed has been a major part in the creation of this book. Donabed has contributed with much of the source material, he has proofread and has been very helpful and encouraging. Without his help, this book would not have come to fruition.

Several other people have, in one way or another, supported me during the course of preparing this book: Sargon George Donabed, Racho Donef, Aryo Makko, Jan Bet-Sawoce, Matay Arsan and Hanibal Romanos. I thank them all sincerely. Needless to say, all shortcomings are my own.   TOMAS BETH-AVDALLA

Contents

Foreword

THERE ARE A variety of treasures in the Modern Assyrian Research Archive (MARA). This is one of them. In the following pages, Tomas Beth-Avdalla has managed to compile a significant amount of texts and photographs concerning the life and works of Dr. Abraham K. Yoosuf, native of Harput (Kharput/Harpoot) in the Ottoman province of Mamuret-ul-Aziz, modern Elazığ. Dr. Yoosuf was perhaps best known for his tireless pursuit of Assyrian recognition during and in the aftermath of the Great War. Furthermore, he is undoubtedly one of the three most significant advocates of what can be termed Assyrianism (or more generally Assyrian culture) from Harput alongside noted Euphrates College Professor Ashur Yoosuf, author of the periodical *Murshid Athuriyun*, as well as philosopher and writer, David Barsum Perley, the focus of volume one in the MARA Collected Texts series.

Few scholars of Middle Eastern history have appreciated the significance of Dr. Abraham K. Yoosuf and his works to the Assyrian community, never mind the notable individual experiences as a combat medic for the Red Crescent Society. Only recently, thanks to MARA, has the door been unlocked to scholars, especially those with an interest in Assyrian Studies. Within the following pages, Beth-Avdalla offers a first look into the mind of a man, beleaguered by duty and desire to aid a benighted community forgotten amidst the rubble in the aftermath of that terrible conflict. It is fitting that my own first experience with the historical Abraham K. Yoosuf comes from a photograph taken during a July 4th 1922 parade on Main Street Worcester, Massachusetts. In the midst of the beginning of a new era in human history, a photograph that displayed a battle-hardened man in military attire and a sign that read "Sons of Assyria" with an Independence Day celebration as the backdrop – a testament to a new kind of Assyrian community.

Perhaps the most significant contribution in the following pages is the collection of the personal notes of Dr. Yoosuf at the Paris Peace Conference in 1919. Imaginably most telling is the previously unobserved inter-Assyrian relationships during the conference, articulated as observed by one of the attendees. The work will create a framework for new discussions of Assyrian politics in the wake of World War I and hopefully, a more nuanced discussion of the type(s) of agency wielded by an indigenous minority in the Middle East as well as in a relatively recent diasporic context, especially in the United States. Perchance this edited collection and future academic inquiry will open the eyes of scholarship to the diverse elements and individuals which made and make up the Assyrian people, and perhaps, in the only case of its kind in the Middle East, go beyond sectarian religious divides, national, linguistic, and economic boundaries, to find common case in an unaccepted, ridiculed, and often reviled heritage.

Sargon George Donabed
Associate Professor of History
Roger Williams University

Introduction

THIS IS THE second book in the MARA Collected Texts series, collecting the known writings of the late Dr. Abraham K. Yoosuf. Despite his short lifetime (58 years), Dr. A. K. Yoosuf managed to accomplish many things. He is best known for his work as Assyrian delegate at the Paris Peace Conference in 1919–1920, where he fought for the rights of the Assyrians and their right to self-determination of Assyria. This is the main content of this book.

The most important document in this book is a unique report prepared by Dr. A. K. Yoosuf during the time he was a negotiator and representative of the Assyrian National Association of America for the Assyrian delegation at the Paris Peace Conference. He describes the day-to-day efforts the delegation made to get the Assyrian voice heard.

Most of the other material included in this book (articles and letters) deals with the same issues and is derived from the same time period.

About the Documents

Sources

The material included in this anthology originates from published and non-published sources such as books, periodicals, pamphlets, documents and letters. These texts were collected by the Modern Assyrian Research Archive (MARA) from the following libraries, publishers, collections and individuals: Mesopotamian Library at Södertörn University (Huddinge, Sweden), ATOUR Publications (USA), George and Elsie Donabed Assyrian Collection (MA, USA), Herbert Basil Quoyoon Assyrian Collection (CT, USA) and Robert Karoukian (CA, USA).

A. K. Yoosuf also wrote and published a book entitled *The Religion of Mohammed and Christian Sufferings*, Worcester 1905, 57 pp.

However, that book has not been included in this anthology, since the book does not deal with Assyrians specifically but with Christians in general.

This anthology is not an archive-in-print. As far as possible, I have tried to include additional notes on the original material. The material has been edited for spelling, grammar, and punctuation. Several personal names are often spelled diffirently and, as far as possible, I have tried to standardize the names. All records have been reformatted and repaginated. Additional editorial notes appear in footnotes and brackets.

Arrangement and selection
The material in this book is arranged chronologically by date of publication based on the information provided in the publication, or in the case of the letters, by the date the letter was signed.

The book is divided into seven parts:

- Articles (Part I)
- Letters (Part II)
- Report to the Executive Committee of the A.N.A. (Part III)
- Statement of Dr. A.K. Yoosuf (Part IV)
- Writings Regarding Dr. A.K. Yoosuf (Part V)
- Digital Images of the Paris Report (Part VI)
- Extracts (Part VII)

This anthology attempts to provide all known and available writings of Dr. A. K. Yoosuf, whether published and found in printed books and periodicals, or not published but found in private collections. However, some single writings in Arabic, Armenian, Eastern Assyrian and Turkish have not been included. (These can be found in the periodicals of *Bethnahrin*, *The Union*, *Izgedda*, *Nineveh* and *Babylon*.)

Tomas Beth-Avdalla
Gothenburg, Sweden
July 2017

Biography of Dr. Abraham K. Yoosuf (1866–1924)[1]

Dr. Abraham K. Yoosuf was born in Harpoot,[2] Turkey, on December 17, 1866.

He attended the Christian Mission School in Harpoot and received his Bachelor of Arts, A.B., at Central Turkey College in Antab, in 1886. He was instructor at Central Turkey College until 1889 when he immigrated to the United States.

He worked his way through Baltimore Medical School, graduating in 1895 with high honors, and began his practice in Worcester, Massachusetts.

In 1897 he organized the Assyrian Benefit Association of which he was president for several years.

He took post-graduate courses in London in 1912, and then left for Vienna, where he studied the diseases of the eye, ear and throat. Upon completion of his studies, he left for Constantinople, arriving just at the outbreak of the Balkan Wars of 1912–13. He immediately volunteered his services and was assigned as a surgeon. He was later decorated by the Sultan of Turkey for his exceptional service, particularly during the cholera epidemic.

When the United States entered the First World War, he immediately enlisted and served his adopted country well, completing his service as a Major.

He spent over two years[3] in Paris and London working in the interests of Assyrians at the Paris Peace Conference.

He took an active part in the building of St. Mary's Assyrian Apostolic Church in Worcester, serving as its first President in 1923.

Dr. Yoosuf was a member of the American Medical Society, the Massachusetts State Society, the Alumni Association in America of the Central Turkey College, and various other societies.

He served his church, his people, and his adopted country unselfishly and was held in high esteem by all who knew him. He died in Worcester on December 26, 1924.

1. Source: *Fiftieth Anniversary St. Mary's Assyrian Apostolic Church Worcester, Massachusetts, Hogan Campus Center, College of the Holy Cross, October 26, 1974,* p. 4. (*Editor*)

2. It is also written as *Harpoot, Kharput* and *Harput.* (*Editor*)

3. He was in Paris (and London) from March 19, 1919 until September 20, 1920. (*Editor*)

Assyrians at a picnic, circa 1900 in Rhode Island, with Dr. A. K. Yoosuf standing in the rear. Some of the individuals have been identified in the photo appear to be written by Mary Arslen, the mother of Phyllis Saffer. (Courtesy of Kasper "Kay" & Phyllis Saffer Family and MARA.)

This photograph of Assyrian men, was taken sometime between 1905 and 1907. Dr. A.K. Yoosuf is seated in the second row, fourth from the left. (Courtesy of Kasper "Kay" & Phyllis Saffer Family and MARA.)

A. K. Yoosuf, A.B., M.D.

Chief Surgeon of Red Crescent Society
at Constantinople, Turkey

Dr. A.K. Yoosuf during his work for the Red Crescent Society at Constantinople, Turkey. 1912–1913 (Courtesy of Kasper "Kay" & Phyllis Saffer Family and MARA.)

Assyrian Benefit Association was established in 1897 and incorporated in 1911 in Worcester, MA. Dr. A. K. Yoosuf is standing in the middle, second row from above with grey jacket and a white hat. This photograph is from 1914. (Courtesy of George & Elsie Donabed Assyrian Collection.)

Worcester, Massachusetts 1922, July 4th parade. Kharput Assyrian participants headed by Dr. A. K. Yoosuf. (Courtesy of Kasper "Kay" & Phyllis Saffer Family and MARA.)

Worcester, Massachusetts 1922, July 4th parade. Kharput Assyrian participants headed by Dr. A. K. Yoosuf. (Courtesy of George & Elsie Donabed Assyrian Collection.)

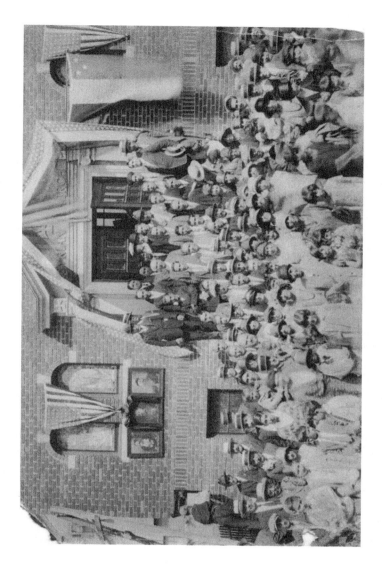

Laying of cornerstone of St Mary's Assyrian Apostolic Church,
Worcester, MA. in August 1925. The ceremony was celebrated by
Rev. Naum Koorie, Rev. Nouri Koorie of New York, Rev. Gabriel
Boyajy of Springfield and deacon G. E. Sugar. Note the photo
of Dr. A. K. Yoosuf on the church wall, between the photos of
Patriarch Elias Shaker III and that of Bishop Aphrem Barsom.
(Courtesy of George & Elsie Donabed Assyrian Collection.)

Dr. A. K. Yoosuf pictured here with his sister Mary Elias and her children George, Stephen and Zerouhy. (Courtesy of George & Elsie Donabed Assyrian Collection.)

PART I

ARTICLES

"

[...] Give them a chance, and they shall prove to the world their ability as fighters, as administrators, as educators. They are the sons and daughters of that mighty Kingdom of Assyria.

Abraham K. Yoosuf (p. 40)

Our Difficulties[4]

THERE ARE MANY signs of awakening among the Assyrians after years of slumber, and the great forces which have worked for dissolution in the past, now seem to me, are working harmoniously together.

There are many difficulties in our path. We are poor in financial as well as in educational ways. We have forgotten the great fundamental principals in this life, which carries a nation forward and brings her in contact with others on the same level – national character and national education.

The majority, in this country and in Turkey, have lost our mother tongue, under pressure of reigning dynasties, and the geographical conditions of the countries have prevented the Assyrians from becoming one and using a uniform language, different tongues are spoken in the different places. This is one of the greatest difficulties confronting us and should be solved by us.

Our ecclesiastics have been so ignorant and indifferent concerning the people that they have left them to their destiny. No schools where our young men can learn and become our leaders and devote themselves to the success of the nation.

Uniformity of our language is an absolute necessity. There must be some way to solve this question. There are many societies, which are endeavoring to do some good for their nation and brethren here. My first suggestion to these societies, would be to accumulate a substantial sum for the educational work. Second, beginning from now on, prepare some young men for better educational work, for there are many worthy young men that hunger for education, and who are willing to do service for their nation. **We need men of education.**

The Assyrian Erootha (or Intibah) Association has taken the greatest step forward for the idea of bringing out the Assyrian civilization,

4. Source: *The New Assyria*, Vol. I, No. 2, October 15 1916, pp. 5, 8. (*Editor*)

her wonderful achievements of literature and science. Old Assyria has been forgotten, with her beauty and heroic works. It is time to bring her glory once more to the forelight, exhibiting her to the civilized nations of the world. We deserve recognition and hope through this medium that the American people will know about the Assyrians.

We have been kept away from the western continent for one reason or the other. Our neighboring and much smaller nation, coming from the same country, has been recognized, and the great mass of Americans knows of them and are very much interested in their cause. Daily papers and magazines write about their sufferings and massacres, while Assyrians are living and suffering under the same conditions. We have no authentic news from our patriarch or his circle to present our cause to the American public for Americans are ready to recognize us if we present our cause and interest them.

"Mass meeting – Union of Turkish and Persian Assyrians. Rev. Werda, speaker, publisher, organiser of 1914–1915 – 15 branches in U.S. The Assyrian National Assn of America. 1. Rev. Joel Werda (P), 2. Prof. Naum Pallak Faik (T), 3. Saleeba Bahoos (T), 4. Senharib Bally (T), 5. Charles S. Dartley (T), 6. Thomas Matloob (T), 7. David Badal (P), 8. George Mardinly (T), 9. Pera Benjamin (P), 10. Hanna Kedersha (T), 11. Rev. Hanna Koorie (T) opposed the unity. N.J. U.S.A. 1914." (Courtesy of George & Elsie Donabed Assyrian Collection.)

It is Well To Mourn
for a Good and Patriotic Man[5]

ASHUR S. YOOSUF, FOREMOST Assyrian in the city of Harpoot, is dead – not dead – but murdered;[6] the Assyrians of that city are crying;

5. Source: *The New Assyria*, Vol. I, No. 3, November 15, 1916, pp. 3, 5. (*Editor*)

6. The tragic last days of Ashur Yoosuf's life are best told by himself:

"Monday April 20, 1915

From my cell to my beloved brother, Hanna Yoosuf in America.

Yesterday on Sunday morning April 19th, 1915 when we had heard that the Turks were crazed with the anger of beastly slaughter, sparing neither man, woman nor child, we became terrified. Especially when the news came of the arrests of my comrades, I began to shiver, and during the course of preparing a hiding place, I myself was arrested and brought to this cell.

This is a good opportunity that I am enjoying to write you my last letter, for I know we will be cut to pieces when we leave here, though I do not know when and where.

Do not worry over my death – it is God's will – I am going to heaven to protect the rights of the Assyrians at the presence of the biggest and greatest Judge. The books and the work I had started about our nation's education remains unfinished. I am afraid they will be destroyed in a very short time. One of my biggest desires has been to keep our brother Donabed away from drink. I'd have given anything under the sun to have made him temperate, but it was in vain. I will give him my last advice after I finish writing to you.

I leave my loving wife and children in your care. My son Isaak was to graduate from high school this year. I had intended to give him a college education, which is another unfinished task I leave in your hands.

The time is almost up, and I close this sad message with wishes for your welfare and safety, so that God may some day lead you to revenge your enemies!

Farewell brother, farewell.

Ashur S. Yoosuf "

Yoosuf and others, among them Barsum Keshish, the late David B. Perley's father,

Ashoor S. Yoosuf. (Courtesy of Jack Petersen and MARA.)

his friends and relatives lament for him, the entire Nation is weeping. The blow is too hard to endure, indeed.

The terrible message was short and conclusive and came to us as a thunderbolt. He is murdered; the noble Assyrian, Ashur S. Yoosuf, was murdered with the rest of the professors.

were taken to the "red prison" where they awaited death. While in prison they were tortured mercilessly. In Document 69 of Lord Bryce's *Treatment of the Armenians in the Ottoman Empire*, it was stated that the hair of his head (Professor Ashur Yoosuf), moustache and beard were pulled out in an attempt to pin a confession of treason against him. He was then starved and hung by his arms for a day and a night, beaten, had his fingernails extracted, his eyes gouged out, and physically stigmatized by the merciless Turks with scalding metal pokers. Source: Donabed, Sargon, *Remnants of Heroes: The Assyrian Experience* (Assyrian Academic Society Press: Chicago, 2003), p. 114. On the Assyrian Genocide in general, see: Gaunt, David, *Massacres, Resistance, Protectors: Muslim-Christian Relations in Eastern Anatolia During World War I* (Gorgias Press: Piscataway, 2006). (*Editor*)

Mr. Ashur S. Yoosuf was born in Harpoot, in 1858 and had received his early education in that city. He was a close friend, associate and relative of the late Rev. A.G. Bedikian.

By the death of Ashur S. Yoosuf, we have lost a literary man, a poet, a publisher, a teacher and above all, a patriot. He has stood for his nation without an apology. He has fought for her on every occasion and was proud of being an Assyrian. I remember him while a student in the Central Turkey College, either debating Assyrian problems or arguing in her favor and defending her against any attack. His dreams and works, his writings and his speeches all were for the Assyrian nation, for her progress and for her civilization. Wherever he went, he never abandoned his nationality for the sake of comfort or for money. I remember well while he was in Malatia he was asked by the Catholics to become a teacher in their school. He occupied the position for a while, but when he found out that there was pressure to make him Catholic, he immediately resigned his position.

He was a fearless fighter for right and justice. He never thought about his person or his living, as his prime object in life was the elevation of his Nation, and her progress. With his mighty pen, he has scorned, many a time, ignorant ecclesiastics for their lack of ability, education and neglect of their sacred duty toward church and community. He has fought the fight alone, without help from his followers. He was a man of strong conviction for certain principles in life and, nothing could induce him in changing his views regarding these principles.

He has given all his time for the welfare of his people and has tried very hard to make them understand the gravity of national existence. He was a paramount spokesman for education. He has traveled to Diyarbakir and Mardin solely for national questions, leaving his work behind, and without compensation. He has done all these for the love of his Nation.

Mr. Ashur S. Yoosuf had a clear and vivid conception on any subject when writing or speaking. He had a rare literary and poetic ability. His Armenian language was splendid, and his literary works have been recognized by the best Armenian authors. He has contributed many literary gems to *Avedaper*, *Purag-Paunch*, and many other Armenian daily and weekly papers. He has received honors and prayers for his literary work. He captured the second prize, given by the late Mr. Tavshanjian of New York, for best article on alcohol. Some years ago, he had a very feverish literary controversy with Mr. Zartarian, a well-known Armenian critic and literary man, who after all, under the caustic and piercing pen of Ashur S. Yoosuf, Mr. Zartarian was obliged to bow and accept his inevitable defeat. Ashur S. Yoosuf was not only a master of the Armenian language, but he spoke Turkish well and fluently. While busy with his work, he studied the Assyrian language also.

He was very anxious to have and edit an Assyrian paper, through which he thought he could serve his fellow countrymen better. He kept the paper, *Murshid* many years without receiving enough money for his labors. He kept it with the hope of having the Assyrian and a

The first page of the first issue of Murshid Athuriyun (Courtesy of Herbert Quoyoon Assyrian Collection and MARA.)

7. *Murshid Athuriyun* was a monthly magazine published in the city of Kharput by the well-known Professor Ashur Yoosuf (1858–1915), who was the editor. It was mainly published in Ottoman Turkish (using Syriac Garshuni script), but some articles and texts included are in Syriac, Arabic and Western Assyrian. According to Sargon Donabed in his *Remnants of Heroes: The Assyrian Experience* (2003), it was in publication for six years until the time of his ordered death. MARA has all issues published from January 1909 to December 1912, all originating from the Herbert Basil Quoyoon Assyrian Collection. (*Editor*)

press for facilitating the work. Before accomplishing this desire, the European war broke out, and during the early deportation and wholesale persecution and murder, he was taken to prison with the rest of his co-workers. We were in hopes to hear his life was spared, and after many anxious months, we received the message, very simple and effective: "There was a good and noble Assyrian, Ashur S. Yoosuf; he was also murdered with the other professors."

Martyr Yoosuf was a student in Central Turkey College. After years of brilliant life in college, he was obliged to leave this educational center to teach. He taught schools in Amasya, Smyrna, Antioch and many other cities. After some years of teaching in Smyrna, he tried to become an Assyrian missionary. For this purpose, he communicated with Mr. Curtis, at Constantinople, who promised to assist him in this matter. Two English prelates, or overseers, started for Aleppo, where Mr. Yoosuf was to meet them, but the unfortunate massacre of 1894–5 and the death of the Assyrian Patriarch[8] set back all the arrangements and future prospects. Since then, he was on the teaching

The city of Harpoot, view from the West. Euphrates College at the left. (Courtesy of MARA.)

staff of Euphrates College. He has been loved by the students and by his associates. He has been a good teacher, noble and sympathetic, forgiving and open-hearted. He has received from the Turkish Bureau of Education a degree of a superior title. Teaching has been his life's work. He loved it, not for the sake of money, but for the work itself

8. i.e. Patriarch Ignatius Peter III [IV] (d. 1894). (*Editor*)

and to have a chance of satisfying his literary ambition and desire.

He has many unpublished articles and poems, which are very valuable indeed. Miss Alice Blackwell, the American talented literary lady, heard of Ashur Yoosuf's poems and wished to translate them to English. What has become of those; what a pity they have perished with him. It will be a great and undying testimony if friends and lovers of his writings were to collect them, whether published or unpublished, and make a living memorial to him.

His family life has been ideal, and relations between husband and wife have been very charming. His wife,[9] a graduate of Euphrates

9. His wife was Arshaluys Oghkasian and their two sons were named Sargon and Isaak. See Donabed, Sargon, *Remnants of Heroes: The Assyrian Experience* (Assyrian Academic Society Press: Chicago, 2003), p. 114. In a letter from Ashur's wife (published in the *Assyrian Progress*, September 1934, p. 4), dated July 3, 1934, in Aleppo, Syria, she writes the following:

"Dear Friend: It was very gratifying to receive such an unexpected letter from you. It awakened some old, old memories within me. It is always pleasant indeed to hear from an old friend that you have almost given up hope of never hearing from.

Dear friend, you can assure my husband's relatives in the United States that I haven't forgotten them. I am always longing to see them and render a little service to them that I could possibly do. But it seems to me it will always be an unpractical desire.

The Harpoot Assyrians here are just the same as they were forty years ago. They live in a separate street under tents. They haven't any schools nor church. They attend the local Assyrian church whose language is Arabic and which they do not understand. The Assyrians from Urfa have their own schools and have intentions to build a church also. The Harpoot Assyrians are in the minority and without a leader.

The patriarchal chair is at Homs now. By chance, I met his Holiness, Patriarch of Antioch [i.e. Patriarch Aphrem Barsom I]. He is very delightful, respectful and honorable. One of our people informed him in my presence that Ashur was a Protestant. His answer was a very remarkable 'I wish you had fifty Ashurs in your community,' he said.

My one great sorrow is that none of my boys followed their father's footsteps. It seems to me that my daughters have inherited their father's mental powers. They are all married now. I have only Maria left to me that was born after her father's death. My intentions were to give her a college education, but I am not financially able to do so.

Many thanks for the 'Assyrian Progress' that you are sending to me.

Very truly yours,

Mrs. A. A. Yoosuf." (*Editor*)

Girls' College, has been a great help to him. He was very good to his brothers and sisters, listening to their troubles, advising and helping them.

He was a good Christian and patriot. He could not endure dis-patriotism and injustice. What has become of his wife and children, we do not know. We hope they are well and safe, as I am sure his son will be able to take his father's place and accomplish the work he had begun.[10]

10. Concerning Ashur S. Yoosuf's son, George, the following news article was published in *The New Beth-Nahreen*, Vol. 5, No. 7, November-December, 1944, p. 20.: "News from Syria and Turkey: The widow of the late Prof. Ashur S. Yoosuf, of Harpoot, Turkey, now in Aleppo, Syria, reports to one of our reporters that her son, George, 40 years of age, suffered death in an explosion in Aleppo, by a steamer. The explosion took place on April 8th last and the injured was transferred to a hospital but was so severely burned that he died att 11.00 P. M. of the same day. George was the main support of the family. Such is the sequence of tragedies. His famous father was killed in Turkey in 1915. We can not think of words that can bring consolation to his bereaved mother. Heaven alone can do so. You have our sincere sympathy, Mrs. Yoosuf, and we weep with you for the tragedies you have so sadly been made to experience!"

Assyria and the Peace Conference[11]

B EFORE THIS WORLD War, the Eastern question was merely a scrap of paper. But with the entry of Turkey into the war, the Eastern question has taken a new phase.

After the Balkan war, the Turkish politicians and military heads were dreaming of new conquests – repossession of her territories – a great country like Egypt, Enver Pasha and his supporters went into this war on the side of Germany, knowing with confidence and utmost belief of German victory, blindly trusting German promises.

This action of Turkey brought about different thoughts of new adjustments of the Near East policy. Had Turkey maintained a neutral attitude during this war, very likely she would have preserved her *status quo*. Turkey's part in this war has lost her all her chances of preserving her possessions and the redeeming of her territories. The Allies will never back those places where they have lost many precious lives and sealed the destiny of the Turkish Empire with Allied blood.

At the early stages of the war, the intention of the Central Powers were alike in seeking the mastery of the situation. The main object of both sides was to win the war, but with the progress of this war, the real objects for which they were fighting gradually revealed themselves to the Allies. The whole world came to realize that this was not a war of conquest but a war of justice. Let me lead you for a while to the countries of the Far East, to Australia, to New Zealand, to India, while to the north, Canada and the magnificent part they played in giving their sons, their wealth, their all, to their cause and their mother country's cause, against those who were fighting for autocracy, against the iron hand that was trying to rule the world, causing ruins,

11. Source: *The New Assyria*, Vol. III, No. 29, January 15, 1918 [1919], pp. 2–3. (*Editor*)

devastation, destitution. Bernhardi and his followers proclaiming that MIGHT IS RIGHT. And that no a weak or small nation has the right to exist. This inhuman declaration gave echo in the hearts of every democratic country, even arousing the American people, re-echoing the voice of this free republic through its president who declared that the weak and small nations have the right to rule themselves.

This most emphatic enunciation in behalf of the smaller nations brought forward the right of the subject nations like Assyria and Armenia. The Armenian question has been before the courts of Europe many years but has never been solved under the Turkish regime. The Assyrians have not experienced so many stormy periods as their neighbors and co-suffering brothers, the Armenians, but nevertheless, they have suffered under the same despotic government of TURKEY. They have tried to keep their existence, fighting against odds. They have been cut off from Europe and America, concerning their sufferings. Have they, the Assyrians, the right of living? Have they the right to demand independence, and autonomy and freedom under a Christian power? The answer is YES. The name of the Assyrian kingdom, her ancient glory, her civilization, science, and literature are known to the world. Assyrians under the despotic government of Turkey have suffered more than any other nation. They have lost their mother tongue. They have suffered massacres and deportations, like her sister nation, the Armenians. In this present war, the Assyrian army has fought for the same cause for which the Allies have fought. First with the Russian army and later with the British Army and later with the British army in Mesopotamia and Persia. Mar Shimun, the late Patriarch of the Assyrian Nestorians was massacred by a notorious Kurdish brigand.[12] His heroic acts will last forever in the annals of history. He was the commander in chief of the Assyrian army. Agha Petros is now commander in chief of the army took up the fighting that Mar Shimun did not finish.

America, and her president is with us, and she with all the other great nations at the Peace Conference, knowing the character of the Turks and the Kurds, will never think of placing the Assyrians under their power.

12. About the murder of Mar Shimun, see: *The Claims of the Assyrians Before the Conference of Peace at Paris*, in this book. (*Editor*)

Mar Shimun and Agha Petros. (Courtesy of MARA.)

The Assyrians are known to Great Britain especially during this war than at any other time. Mesopotamia, that beautiful fertile country, the Paradise of the East, the center of ancient civilization, is now under her control. She will never yield them to Turkey again. That government who joined hands with the Huns in spite of the great favors which the English had shown the Turks during the past. England will never forget the crimes the Turkish government has committed against its Christians time and time again. She has no fear from Russia or Germany.

The Assyrians demand Mesopotamia for it is the cradle of the Assyrian nation, and she is ready to possess it once more under the protectorate of the British Government, proving to her and also to all the other great powers that she, Assyria, can govern herself. The Assyrians of Persia, Turkey, America, Syria, India, and all over the world are ready to sacrifice their all for the freedom of their mother country. They want to see again their flag floating over the fertile lands of Beth Nahreen [Mesopotamia].

The Christian nations under the Turkish rule demand their rights of self government. It is time to organize a federal union of the Assyrians, Armenians and Syrians in Turkey and Persia and with a strong voice, demand justice at the Peace Conference.

Mesopotamia and England[13]

T HERE ARE VARIOUS opinions concerning Mesopotamia and her future. The King of Hedjaz has already uttered his words before the Peace Conference in regard to that region, claiming the Arabian control. The world is cognizant of Arab's historical civilization of the past centuries, but, nevertheless, Arabs possess the same religion as Turks, the same Koran as Turks, and the same belief and doctrine as Turks and the same feeling toward their Christian subjects.

The great objection of this proposed union of Christians and Mohammedans will be on the religious basis. Those who have studied the teachings of Islam can instantly recognize the difficulty, impossibility, and injustice of such a union. The Turkish Empire has proven my statement in regard to the treatment of Christian Nations. Though there are some subject Christians speaking the Arabic language, this alone will not give the right of claiming union. The religious differences, political understandings, national characteristics of Arabic, the affairs of those nations and adjusting them, race cannot assimilate the Christians into an Arabic nation. The religion in the Far East is a *great* factor which requires attention. Arabs have been subjects to Turkey, as other nations, like Assyrians and Armenians. Though they possess Arabic subtility but never will know *political training*, no *statesmanship*, no idea of *governing* the *people*, no civilization of high type, no universal education, no tolerance. They have never held any high official position in either State affairs or in military defenses in the Turkish Government. How could it be possible to give Mesopotamia to an Arab nation, when she is unable to establish a government without the knowledge of the fundamentals of democracy.

To establish a successful government and continue it, is an important question. The Arab is lacking the ability of governing and

13. Source: *The New Assyria*, Vol. III, No. 31, March 15, 1919, pp. 9–10. (*Editor*)

controlling the subject people. They have not proved to the world their ability as a governing nation – a nomadic nation cannot control and govern a civilized community in Mesopotamia.

No government or even Peace Conference can sell or give the rights of a nation to another. The people have the right of declaring their intention before such a step could be taken. Each nation, no matter how small it may be, has the right of living, and living free. This is the declaration of the Allied Powers.

The people in Mesopotamia can alone decide this question. England alone has the right to say and to decide the fate of Assyrians living there. All Assyrians, whether living in Mesopotamia or elsewhere, desire to establish an independent state along modern lines, if possible, under either mandate of the British Government or of the United States of America. Great Britain has a very great and a peculiar interest in that part of the Orient. She has been fighting there since the beginning of the war, making great sacrifices in men and money, bringing deliverance to the people of Mesopotamia. The Assyrian mountaineers in Kurdistan, in Midyat, and Urmia have fought for the cause of the Allies, defending their country and homes from cruel attacks of combined Turks, Kurds, and Persians, driving the enemies everywhere. When the Persian Government demanded their arms, the answer was, "the free Christian mountaineers never surrender." They have not surrendered to Turkey and will not surrender to Persia.

They have fought for their freedom, their women have fought for their sanctity against the cruelty of the Kurds and Turks, and often throwing themselves into the rivers and killing themselves to escape from the persuading mobs. Today the British Government is feeding 150–160 thousand of refugees escaped and departed from Urmia and Mesopotamia to the region of Bagdad.

British troops are in that land now, and the people have the confidence in her justice, tolerance, and freedom. The people of Mesopotamia and Urmia wish to see the English flag floating over there with the flag of Assyria until the Assyrians prove their loyalty to their deliverer, to exhibit their sagacity, ability of self-government, then England will give Mesopotamia to the Assyrians to establish a new government.

Assyrians from America and from Mesopotamia will appear before the tribunal to plead their cause and to demand their rights – justice, reparation, freedom. They need the sympathy and the help of the world, as they have suffered having been murdered, massacred, and tortured just the same way as her neighbor, the Armenians.

Give them a chance, and they shall prove to the world their ability as fighters, as administrators, as educators. They are the sons and daughters of that mighty Kingdom of Assyria.

A Remark or Two
Concerning the Near East[14]

THE TIME IS near when the democratic governments of the West will seriously consider the question of the Near East. The Supreme Council of the World Peace Conference is trying to solve the difficulty and complicated problems of the Near East – yes, trying to determine that this war be the last war. It will not be the last war unless they adjust the affairs rightly and use the Allied victory in such a way so as to remove certain causes of war.

Only a mere preaching of goodwill, the ideals of democracy, the wearing out of humanity from this present war and the economical conditions of the belligerent countries will not be sufficient to prevent war in the future.

The Near East has been the scene of continual invasions, ebbing and flowing for centuries. The country has been saturated by continual bloodshed. The moral fortitude of the Christians alone have stood against the tides of extremists and have heroically kept in existence through all the centuries until this day.

The Assyrian hope does not see any Mongul or Tamerlane hordes sweeping across their country. They hope there will not be crusades or jihads. Neither will the massacres, pillaging and deportations be committed by the Turks.

At present, every man with average intelligence in Europe and in America has some knowledge about Turkey. He is aware of the strategic importance of Constantinople. He knows also that the Christians in Turkey have been misgoverned for centuries. That Assyria is a fertile land, food producing land; he knows of the Straits. He remembers the name of Gallipoli. The sacred city of Jerusalem. The Berlin-Bagdad railway. The Bosphorus. The Sea of Marmara. In all, he knows the Turks and their beautiful capital.

14. Source: *The New Assyria*, Vol. III, No. 34, June 15, 1919, pp. 1–3. (*Editor*)

Why has Turkey lived so long? Some years ago his death sentence was uttered by European statesmen. Even by Gladstone, who called him the sick man of Europe. But nevertheless, he has lived long enough to demonstrate once more to the world and prove that he is still able to persecute and massacre the Christians – torture their wives, murder their innocent children and deport them to the deserts of Arabia.

There have been two reasons for his living. First, for the jealousy of the European powers which has been existent among them many years concerning Turkey, and the Straits. Second, the Turkish Government realizing the above fact has for the last half century been playing a clever diplomatic game with the European powers, to one giving the privileges of the railways and to another mortgaging the resources of the country.

Finance and intrigue have played a great role in the past. The European Governments have been caring for this sick man for more than half a century. The Turk has been holding Constantinople because no one nation dares to trust another with so great a prize. Whether the Peace Conference decides that the sultan will reside at Constantinople or not is a matter of consequence. The Allied democracy must be responsible for the fair way. They must have a strong power on sea which will put its authority beyond all doubt.

It is not time for this and similar suggestions. This war has proven exclusively that Turkey's power must come to an end in Asia. The question then naturally will arise. What will become of the Christians in Turkey? To redeem them from the bondage of the Turks and give them autonomy under the European power for a period. Second, do not let Turkey dominate Constantinople, Dardanelles, and the Bosphorus. The present indications of the Allies' intention toward the solution of the Turkish Empire is right. Dismemberment. This is the only solution. This political cancer must be cut off. This is the only cure.

Constantinople and the Dardanelles should be made international. If the Allies expect peace in the Near East, the old financial and economic system must be abolished. Concessions, loans, exploitations, etc., should be decided in the open by a body of persons who command the respect of the world.

Reforms under the Turkish rule must be dismissed as hopeless. The history for the last hundred years has been a history of reforms written in the blood of the Assyrians. Their massacres, deportations, and inprisonments are the proofs of exterminations of the Assyrians. But the hand of Providence has been working against such an abominable policy.

The beautiful land of Assyria which is, and will be, a food producing country with an immense future for agriculture, has been laid waste. Under any rule and with any population but that of the Turk, it would be a paradise.

The Turks may claim and maintain a Turkish state and promise real guarantees for the lives and the properties of the Assyrians, but such a claim cannot be accepted. The past centuries promises and reforms have been a failure. The Assyrians have been crushed under the heels of injustice and barbarism committed by the Kurds. The Kurdish chiefs have been encouraged and decorated for their wrong deeds by the Turkish Government. The very same Kurds, the enemies of the Assyrians who have destroyed their sanctuaries, demolished their properties and live upon the labor of the Assyrian populace. The Kurds who have fought against democracy of the Allied powers, are demanding freedom.

To permit Turkey to occupy his original state, to create a new Kurdish state, and to establish an Arab kingdom will be one of the greatest misfortunes for the Assyrians residing among them.

The Assyrians in Turkey and Persia have fought the Allied battle, sacrificing everything, saturating the earth with their blood for the sake of emancipation and liberty, and for the sake of the land in which they live. The national revival of the nomad Kurd and the retarded Arab of the desert will not be able to throw away their old nature. It will take years to educate and cultivate them, while the Assyrians are ready to follow the path of democracy. They are ready to adopt Western civilization. The Kurds have stood as a barrier against civilization, against humanity. Those who have fought against Christian institutions, today they are demanding recognition before the great tribunal of the world.

Many years the Balkan countries have menaced and threatened the European peace by uncontrolled and uneducated nations among them. It will be the same thing in Asia and Mesopotamia with the nomad and uneducated Kurd. They will be a menace to the safety of the population, unless a strong hand governs them for a long period. When the Assyrians become the master of their own country, when given them the chance of establishing a government built upon the principles of justice and equality, the Kurds and the Turks alike will enjoy the freedom of the government. They will be a part of the government with all the privileges of education. They will alike share the benefit.

Give the Assyrians the chance in Mesopotamia. They will be able to establish a government by the people and for the people. There are men and resources of wealth in that fertile land to bring forth and show to the world the possibilities in Assyria.

What is it All About?[15]

IT SEEMS TO me there is commotion and excitement among Assyrians, or I may say among a party of Assyrians who are elated and making a capital of nothing. Generally, I do not like to answer to such bombastic and empty declarations, and news – but realizing its effect upon some people who are easily deceived and easily lead regardless of facts and truths.

It has been my wish to see Assyrians all united under **one flag**, under **one name**, under **one purpose** and work for the salvation of our nation, regardless of personal benefits and personal ambitions. It shall not be a union until every Assyrian leader works faithfully for the cause, until the leaders give up their habit of filling their pockets with almighty dollars, under the **cover of a nation** and her sufferings. It is a crime unpardonable.

I do not know what this fuss is about. I have read in the *Assyrian Herald*[16] the "great doing" of the delegates from Urmia. Poor souls,

15. Source: *Izgedda – Assyrian American Courier*, Vol. 5, No. 1, October 8 1919, p. 3. (*Editor*)

16. The *Assyrian American Herald* was the second Assyrian periodical to be published in the United States, and it was the first weekly Assyrian newspaper to be published anywhere. Its editor and publisher was Paul S. Newey (1885–1960) who immigrated to the United States in 1906 and eventually went to Chicago to study at the Chicago Theological Seminary where he received a B.D. degree in 1913. He founded the Assyrian Congregational Church in Chicago in 1919 which he served until his passing in 1960. In July 1915, he published the *Assyrian American Herald* which was handwritten. By October 1915, the paper appeared in type designed by Newey. The *Herald* continued for almost six years (until May 1921) and provides an important source of information about the history of the Assyrians during WWI, their struggle for national survival and the challenges they faced in adjusting to life in the diaspora. (*Editor*)

how easily you are fooled. If I was not in Paris and did not know the things very closely, I would keep silent, but when I know it all, I can not keep silent any longer for those unjustly remarks and applauds upon the heads of those heroes from Urmia.

I am surprised to know that they have the audacity of writing their work toward suffering Urmia and Salmas, I do not see any reason for blowing their horns so loudly without giving credit to the rest of the delegates who are working hard constantly for the past months. I do not know **what they have done**. I have been with them a few times, attending their conversations. They have called upon some gentlemen who actually have no influence about arranging the matter. On one occasion, when one of the delegates asked some kind of protection for Assyrians in Urmia, he answered that the demand is impracticable and impossible until we know who is going to be the mandate of those countries, adding also that the Urmia question can not be dealt with separately. When asked again to send the Assyrians to their homes, the gentleman said "Why do not the Assyrians go to Mesopotamia."

Yes, we are in harmony as far as our claim concerns, only their petition has been for Urmia and Salmas for immediate relief. This petition has nothing to do with the **Peace Conference**, as it is a demand for relief. So, I have been to see the American Commissioners, Mr. Morgenthau and Mr. Hoover and others, for providing some means to help those Assyrian sufferers, **not those gentlemen from Urmia and Caucasia**.

If I mention the names of gentleman of high rank, it will fill a page.

Presenting a petition does not accomplish a great thing, as one American delegate told me, "Your people give many claims and petitions."

I do not know, but I doubt if those delegates have seen men of high ranking personalities either American, British, French or Italian. To put the Assyrian question before them and discuss the matter with them. I have done it, and confess it very humbly.

Urmia, is not and cannot represent the whole nation.

Permit me to inform our Assyrian brothers that we – Mr. Werda and myself, as part of Assyrian delegation for the suffering Assyrians in Persia. We had a stormy interview with His Excellency Mirza Hassain Khan Alai, member of the Persian delegation, and still our

Joel E. Werda. (Courtesy of MARA.)

brother Assyrians from **Urmia** accuse us that we have not claimed **Urmia**, etc. Read our **claims**.[17]

We have been working and silently. One of our respectful delegates from America told me "Dr. you are the best hard working man."

I do not see then how a person can deliberately come before the public and blow only his own horn, either such things fabricated there, or else there is a gross mistake on the part of our delegates presenting the matter in a different light.

It is good to be honest in all our dealings, have been honest with them, and I am expecting the same from them.

Very likely the interview and petition to Mr. Pichon has some influence upon our people across the ocean. If the name has an effect, I may mention many names, which have more effects. I have seen him some months ago. Mr. Pichon's answer is in my possession, absolutely it is nothing but an acknowledgement.

Oh well; let me mention some names, that I had the honor of interviewing. Our State Sec. Mr. Robert Lansing, Mr. Arthur Curtis

17. For *The Claims of the Assyrians Before the Conference of Peace at Paris*, see the article following this one. (*Editor*)

James, Mr. Bueler, Prof. [William Lynn] Westermann, American delegates, Sec. of Mr. House, Sir Robert Cecil, Sir Arthur Heartget, Major Gribon and Signor [Tommaso] Tittoni, etc.

We have come here to work not to praise ourselves. Let the people be our judges for our work and our conduct.

Major A. K. Yoosuf, M. D.

Rep. Assyrian delegate from America.

Sept. 11, 1919.

The Claims of the Assyrians Before
the Conference of Peace at Paris[18]

I. THE ASSYRIAN PEOPLE

The Assyrians are better known by their three ecclesiastical designations representing the three main religious bodies of the people. Of these three main divisions:

(A) The **Nestorians** have predominated in the Kurdistan mountains, inhabiting Barwar, Tyari, Tkhooma, Baz, Jeloo, Gawar etc., with Koodchanis as their patriarchal see.

(B) The **Chaldeans** predominate in the province of Mosul, abounding also in the various locations in lower Mesopotamia down to the Persian gulf, with Mosul as their patriarchal see.

(C) The **Jacobites** prevail in the province of Diyarbakir, abounding also in Syria proper, and in other localities in the former empire of Turkey, with the city of Mardin as their patriarchal see.

A careful examination of the various statistics compiled by the European experts as to the Assyrian population shows that the resources from which they were compelled to draw were entirely erroneous and misleading. This error, in all probability, is largely due to the fact, that a very large number of the Assyrians lost their mother tongue and speak Turkish, Arabic and Armenian, and the Armenian speaking Assyrians became identified with the Armenian people and were counted as Armenians. Thus, during the so called Armenian massacre and exile, fully 175,000 Assyrians perished, and were listed under the Armenian atrocities.

Exclusive of the three main Assyrian divisions mentioned above, there are also:

(D) The Assyrian Maronite element. The **Maronite** Assyrians became identified with their Syrian co-religionists and are

18. Source: *Izgedda – Assyrian American Courier*, Vol. 5, No. 2, October 15 1919, p. 3. (*Editor*)

erroneously named to the present day as the "Syrians."

(E) The **Persian Assyrians**. Before the war broke out, the city and the district of Urmia alone claimed 82,000 Assyrians who occupied 112 villages. The small district of Salmas claimed 10,000 Assyrians. Settled in the various cities and localities on the western boundary of Persia, immediately adjoining Turkey, there have lived about 150,000 Assyrians.

(F) The **Assyrians** in **Russia**. Driven by the Mohammedan oppression, large numbers of the Assyrians had left both Persia and Turkey to settle in the various parts of south Russia. Some 30,000 to 40,000 of these sojourn now in the district of Yerevan, Caucasia. A similar number is at the present time in the city of Tiflis and its environs, in Caucasia. Other Assyrians formed temporary settlements situated on the Black Sea. During the first Russian withdrawal from Azerbaijan, about 40,000 Persian Assyrian refugees managed to escape to Russia and have remained there since. All told there are not less than 100,000 Assyrians in Russia. 95 percent of these are ready to return to an autonomous state, freed from former oppression, and protected by some mandatory power.

The most conservative figures will place the Assyrian population at not less than 600,000 (not including India and Egypt Assyrians). And while the three main Assyrian bodies are separated from each other by certain areas occupied by the non Assyrian elements, they nevertheless are living in a proximity sufficiently close to form a separate state protected by some mandatory power.

(G) The **Islamic Assyrians**. Like unto the ruins which tell the story of a past catastrophe, the Moslemized Assyrians constitute to which the Assyrian people for centuries have been subjected. Within the areas still occupied by the Assyrians, or in the immediate vicinity of all such areas, there are Moslems which are distincly of Assyrian origin. Perhaps one or two examples should suffice, not only to reveal this fact, but also to show the justification of both the Assyrian claims and the Assyrian aspirations.

In a portion of the Kurdistan mountains, immediately west of the Persian boundary, there has lived a Kurdish tribe of considerable size, known by the name of "Shakkak," who themselves admit their Assyrian nationality, and to the present day they address the Nestorian patriarch in the most reverent manner, calling him by an endearing designation of "Uncle."

In the district of Sapna, immediately above the district of Barwar, in upper Mesopotamia, there are bodies of Kurds, still retaining sufficient characteristics to prove their Assyrian origin.

The Yazidis of the Sinjar mountains, numbering now more than 300,000 souls, are of the Assyrian blood, relatively recent date.

It is not necessary to make mention of similar bodies in other localities, but the leaders of the Assyrian people have always looked for the day of opportunity to reclaim their lost nationals back into the Christian faith and also into the national fold. And, indeed, with this end in view the Assyrian National Associations have been organized, not only in the United States and Canada, but also elsewhere. Funds have been collected, and national treasuries have been created with sufficient resources to establish national schools, not only for the Assyrian people, but also those of their brethren in flesh and blood who are now lost to them in the fold of Islam. And surely, history shows, that the Assyrians, when given an opportunity, are capable of the achievement.

II. THE ASSYRIANS AND THE WAR[19]

After the entry of the Russian forces into Persia, and immediately before the declaration of war by Turkey, the Turkish government sent official emissaries to Mar Shimun, the patriarch of the Nestorian branch of the Assyrian people and offered the late patriarch large sums of money in gold on the condition that the patriarch and his people should remain neutral. Of the three Assyrian patriarchs, Mar Shimun alone was in a position to strike against the Turks with the Assyrian independent tribes of Tyari, Tkhooma, Baz and Jeloo. In the meanwhile, Mar Shimun's brother, who was studying in Constantinople, was kept as a hostage by the Turkish government and threatened with a horrible death, in case Mar Shimun refused the Turkish offer and went over to the side of the Allies. This intelligence was officially communicated to the head and the leader of the Nestorians. The patriarch, however, sent envoys to the Russian military authorities in Urmia, Persia, by whom he had previously been approached and from whom he had received a promise of 25,000 guns and informed the latter that he had decided to declare war against Turkey.

19. Source: *Izgedda – Assyrian American Courier*, Vol. 5, No. 3, October 22 1919, p. 3. (*Editor*)

In addition to the Turkish offer, the German consul in Mosul sent agents to Mar Shimun, guaranteeing the absolute security of all the Assyrians in the Turkish Empire on the condition of the patriarch's neutrality. Even this German offer was refused, and the hostilities commenced between the Turks and the Nestorian Assyrians.

Thus, from the time of Turkey's entry into the war, the Assyrians have fought incessantly as a distinct unit in the group of the Allied Nations. The victories credited to the Russian forces in Kurdistan were in reality won by the Assyrian forces in that front of battle. The Kurds, who were a perpetual menace to the Russian operations, were absolutely cleared from those valleys by the army of Mar Shimun. And had the Russians fulfilled their promise of supplying the patriarch's forces with rifles and a few cannon, the capture of Mosul by the Assyrians would have been an easy possibility.

However, surrounded on all sides by vastly superior numbers, short of guns and ammunition, face to face with total extermination because of their siding with the Allies, sacrificing thousands on the field of battle, and losing tens of thousands through actual starvation and disease, the Assyrians never faltered. Through all the vicissitudes and the turning tides of the war, and after the collapse of Russia, the Nestorian Assyrians remained loyal to their Allies, and endured all for the sake of the freedom of all the Assyrians.

The independence which they now seek, they do not ask as a charity, they demand it by appealing to the sense of justice and equity. They have fought for it; they have purchased it with the streams of their own blood shed on the field of battle. In Kurdistan, in Turkey, in Persia, in Russia, in Poland and in France, lay the graves of the Assyrians, which stand not only as splendid monuments to their valor, but also as a tremendous price paid for the restoration of their lands, and for the independence of their people. Even the late patriarch himself laid down his life upon the altar of his people's freedom.

A nation that has lost nearly one third of its numerical strength because of the part it played in the World War, must surely be entitled to recognition and independence, especially in the presence of those political declarations which have repeatedly proclaimed the inauguration of a new era, wherein the principle of self determination was to be recognized as a sacred and inherent right of mankind.

III. THE TERRITORIAL CLAIMS OF THE ASSYRIANS

The original land of the Assyrians embraced an area of 250,000 square miles. Islamic power seized the land, and planted Islamic elements in the newly confiscated territory. The name, however, with whatever dialect pronounced, stands as an eternal deed, showing that the house belongs to the Assyrians. And no tribunal of justice can overlook this fact. The Assyrians, however, do not pretend to claim all this original territory. But they do claim that portion of upper Mesopotamia, where they abound in large numbers. This portion of the land embraces naturally an area which stretches from below the lower Zab, up to and including the province of Diyarbakir, where the Assyrians vastly outnumber the Armenians; and also from the Euphrates in the west to the mountains of Armenia in the east. Added to this, the Assyrians naturally desire an access to the sea.

The Assyrians realize that in all probability the Kurdish elements, which reside in the area claimed by them, may present a sort of problem that will command attention. Against such a possible observation, we feel that we must present the following memorandum:

1. Morally there cannot be discrimination between the Kurds and the Turks. The Kurd proved himself just as an efficient a tool for the aspirations of an imperial Germany, as did the Turks, while the former vastly exceeded the latter in ferocity and brutality against all the Christians, and particularly against the Assyrians. The crime of one is the guilt of the other.

2. To place an enemy element, which happens to be dwelling in the area claimed by the Assyrians, on the same level with a people that has suffered and suffered gladly and so heavily in the Allied cause, would be, to place the criminal on the same level with the innocent, and it would mean lasting injustice to the Assyrians.

3. While it is perhaps just that even the Kurds, as a race, are entitled to the benefits of the principle of self determination, if they so desire, but to permit their claim to expand and infringe upon the exclusive of the Assyrians, is to place a premium on plunder, murder and massacre.

4. So long as there exist religious bigotry and religious fanaticism, and the word "Gavoor" (heathen) is not eliminated from the vocabulary of the Turk or of the Kurd, this Islamic element can never be trusted by the Assyrians. The wild beast is now caged by defeat and

not tamed by culture. In order to free the Assyrians from the repetition of the former barbarities to which they have been subjected for centuries by the combined hatred of the Turk and the Kurd, and in order to save their position from being exposed to the previous perils, the reasonable area thus claimed by them, even though including some Kurds within its bounds, must be created into an Assyrian state under the protectorate of some mandatory power.

5. It would be decidedly to the moral, educational and spiritual advantage of those Kurds, who will thus remain in a newly created Christian state, to receive the benefits of those educational and industrial enterprises which the Assyrians themselves have undertaken to establish.

6. It will be decidedly in the interest of peace, at least in that portion of Asia, as well as to the advantage of the power holding the mandatory authority in the land, and also to the moral and spiritual advantages of all the non Christian and heterogenous elements of the entire Mesopotamia, to grant to the Assyrians the new state they desire and embracing the area they claim.

Has the agony of the war given birth to the rights of mankind? If so, the awful sacrifices made, meet their equal compensation. Anything short of the righteous and reasonable claim of a people, no matter how weak or how small, is bound to bring another day of retribution. Heaven with sorrow witnessed the tragedy of the war; it now hearkens with yearning to the cry of the small nations and looks with longing for the enactment of justice to the oppressed people. Therefore, immeasurably greater than the crisis of the war, are those which now hang upon the treatment accorded to the weak and the deserving.

IV. THE CLAIMS OF THE ASSYRIANS FOR REPERATION.[20]

A ruthless slaughter of innocent women and children cannot be condoned. A deliberate crusade, to exterminate one whole nation, cannot be concealed under the cover of an unconditional surrender. If Turkey failed to exterminate the remainder of the Assyrian and confiscate their property, she did so because she failed in her war. She, perhaps, can never pay for all the material and other losses suffered by

20. Source: *Izgedda – Assyrian American Courier*, Vol. 5, No. 4, October 29, 1919, p. 3. (*Editor*)

the Assyrians under her most oppressive rule for centuries, but for the losses inflicted upon the Assyrians during the war, both Turkey and Germany should be compelled to make reparation. Fully 200,000 Assyrians of the Kurdistan valleys and plains are absolutely deprived of everything they owned, and their homes are left in ruins. In order that they may be able to rehabilitate themselves, they should be compensated for their entire material losses. And likewise, we believe ourselves entitled to reparation for all the Assyrians who resided in the interior of Turkey.

The Assyrians in the district of Diyarbakir, including Urfa, Harpoot, Mardin and Midyat, have passes through a literal deluge of blood. The Assyrian population was put to the edge of the sword by the regular troops of Turkey. The villages including those in the district of Bohtan were totally destroyed. Altogether, more than 186,000 men, women and children were massacred. 84 Jacobite churches and 14 monasteries were razed to the ground, and 186 Assyrian priests were killed in the most barbarous manner.

The brave Assyrian city of Midyat stood the onslaught of the Turkish troops for a period of six months. The city, at last, had to surrender on account of the lack of ammunition and the Turks, besides killing the Assyrian defenders, they have bayonetted every woman and child within the walls. The Assyrian city of Midyat is a heap of ruins now.

V. THE CLAIMS OF THE PERSIAN ASSYRIANS.

The Assyrian atrocities in Azerbaijan have equalled, if not surpassed, those inflicted upon their brethren in Turkey. While the Russians were still in Urmia, the local Mohammedans had caught the echo of Turkey's proclamation of the "holy war," and they were then seeking an opportunity to pour out their vengeance upon the defenseless Assyrian Christians. This opportunity presented itself, when immediately after the first withdrawal of the Russian forces from Urmia, the entire Mohammedan population arose, lifting up the banner of the *jehad*, and determined to exterminate the entire Christian population of Urmia, Sooldooz, Margavar and Targavar. The Assyrians of the last three named districts had already escaped into Urmia from fear of the approaching Turkish forces. The Assyrians, from all directions, naturally, endeavored to reach the city of Urmia where they might seek the protection of the American and the French flags, which were flying over the buildings of the two respective missions. The Assyrians, however, who had left all their possessions behind, were intercepted by their armed Mohammedan neighbors and killed in the most brutal manner. Old men and women, who were unable to undertake the journey, were either thrown alive into the wells and covered with dirt, or else burned alive in their homes which were set on fire. Little girls, six and eight years of age, were assaulted on open Bibles and on the pulpits of the Christian churches. The leading Assyrians were grouped together, placed in rows, and then either shot by rifles, or beheaded by the sword. The murderers, in a number of instances, actually licked the blood off their swords and daggers to appease their hatred and satisfy their thirst for the blood of the Christians. About 30.000 to 40.000 managed, in a most miraculous way, to reach the city, where they found the American and the French Mission buildings open to receive them. Here they were obliged to remain for several months in a state of siege, and thousands of them perished from contagion and disease.

After the return of the Russian forces into Urmia, the Siberian regiments, as they beheld the atrocious deeds perpetrated upon the Assyrians, they actually shook with emotion and prepared to bombard the city and avenge the blood of the innocent people. It was again the Christians who interceded with the Russian officers, and persuaded them not to return evil for evil.

After the collapse of Russia, the Mohammedan population of Urmia, unmindful of the forgiving spirit shown them previously by the Assyrians and of the desire of the latter for peace and harmony in spite of their losses, rose up once more, this time assisted by the Persian Kurds and the Mohammedans of Salmas. Fortunately, some of the mountain Assyrians, under the leadership of the late Nestorian patriarch, were now in Urmia. The Nestorian patriarch at this time sent two letters, one to the governor of Urmia and the other to the governor general of Azerbaijan at Tabriz, informing them that the Assyrians had absolutely no evil designs, that they were friendly to the Persian Government and begged the governors to prevent the Mohammedan uprisings and also to allow the Assyrians to remain temporarily in Urmia, till God in His mercy showed them a way of escape, either to Caucasia, or to Bagdad. Instead of heeding this request, the two govenors mentioned, had themselves planned the uprising as it became evident later, and were determined on the extermination of the Christian population. The subsequent assassination of the late Mar Shimun, was also a plot which was originally laid in the city of Tabriz. We have the most conclusive proofs to show that the responsibility for the Assyrian massacres and losses in Persia rests absolutely upon the Azerbaijan authorities of Persia. Fully 112 Assyrian villages were burned to the ground or otherwise destroyed. The homes of all the Assyrians in Urmia were plundered, and the household effects, together with the cattle of the Assyrians can be found in the possession of Urmia Mohammedans. The proofs of this responsibility have already been submitted by the leaders of the Assyrian people to the legations of the Allied Nations in Teheran. Fully 50.000 Persian and mountain Assyrians perished because of these fanatical uprisings, and about 4.000 Assyrian women are now kept in bondage in the homes of the Moslems. And during their last exodus from Urmia, on their way to Bagdad, the Assyrians were pursued and shot down by a Majid-el-Saltana, a general in the Persian army.

For the shedding of innocent blood and the material losses they have suffered, the Assyrians present their claim for indemnity against the Azerbaijan government of Persia.

If we were to figure at the shocking rate of 250 toomans which was the standard price allowed by the courts of Urmia for the killing of a Christian by a Mohammedan, the Azerbaijan Government should be held responsible to the extent of 12.500.000 toomans as an indemnity for a deliberate plan to exterminate all the Assyrians and for the actual loss of 50.000 men, women and children.

Indemnity for the Assassination of the Nestorian Patriarch.[21]

The assassination of the late Patriarch Mar Shimun was a most cowardly deed perpetrated by the instigation and conspiracy of the two Persian Governors to whom we have alluded. The Governor General of Azerbaijan, showing apparently compliance with the request of the Assyrian patriarch as contained in his official letter, sent messengers to the latter, asking him to meet the Persian envoys in

21. Source: *Izgedda – Assyrian American Courier*, Vol. 5, No. 5, November 5, 1919, p. 3. (*Editor*)

Salmas, to which place the said envoys were coming from Tabriz. Mar Shimun, accompanied by 200 of his men, and intensely desirous of harmony, left for Salmas. Here in the city of Deliman he met the Persian envoys, entirely ignorant of the fact that their apparent friendship was a mere mask for murder. Most cordial greetings were exchanged, and the negotiating parties apparently came to a mutual understanding. At the conclusion of the interview, the patriarch prepared to depart for Urmia. The Persian envoys, however, suggested that he should also meet Simkoo, a Kurdish brigand and chieftain of a notorious Kurdish tribe, who was also residing then in Salmas. The patriarch replied that Simkoo did not represent the Persian authorities, and he was also not a law abiding Persian subject, and therefore, he could have no dealings with him. The Persian envoys, however, appealing to the patriarch's desire for peace and tranquility and under the pretense of wishing to calm the disturbances in the entire district, insisted that Mar Shimun should visit the notorious Kurdish chieftain. In a spirit of meekness and humility and with a desire to please the Tabriz authorities, the patriarch consented to do so. In the meanwhile, Simkoo, with the full knowledge and deliberate planning of the Tabriz envoys, had his sharp shooters placed in advantageous points on the roofs of the houses adjoining his residence. So when the interview with the Kurdish brigand was over, and as the patriarch emerged from the house into the courtyard where his men were waiting for him, he was received with a rain of bullets, and only six of his wounded attendants managed to escape to tell the story of conspiracy and murder.

Justice demands that the Azerbaijan Government should pay an indemnity of one million toomans for this cowardly betrayal of trust, and for this deliberate plan of assassination and murder.

For the material losses of the Assyrians in Urmia, Salmas, Soldooz, Targavar and Margavar, the Assyrians demand an additional and a most reasonable indemnity of 18.000.000 toomans, making a total of 31,500,00 Toomans, which they justly claim from the Azerbaijan Government of Persia.

The Assyrians desire further to make known the following facts:

1. The districts of Targavar and Margavar, immediately west of the district of Urmia, are almost exclusively inhabited by the Assyrians, while their very names are indicative of Assyrian origin.

2. In the district of Urmia, about 112 villages are almost exclusively inhabited by the Assyrians.

3. In the small district of Salmas, nearly 30 villages are inhabited by the Assyrians and the Armenians mixed.

4. In Somoi and Bradost, immediately north of the district of Targavar, both the Assyrians and the Armenians abound, while part of the Kurdish element in the valley, even though Mohammedan by religion, is of Assyrian blood and origin.

5. The remainder of the population, both in Urmia and in Salmas districts, is not of Persian blood but of Turkish or Afshar origin.

6. Because of the ill and bitter feelings created, first by the pre-war oppression of the Assyrians and then intensified by the fearful outrages perpetrated against them during the war, the interests of peace and harmony can perhaps be best served by an exchange of these districts for some other place which falls within the zone claimed by the Assyrians and which could be more desirable and of decidedly greater advantage to Persia.

The Assyrian delegates would be willing to debate their claim with the Persian delegates, or to enter into negotiations with them for a satisfactory solution of the problem.

VI. THE CAPABILITIES OF THE ASSYRIANS.[22]

The prospect of a people can best be seen in the light of its retrospect. Entirely indifferent to the imperial grandeur of the bygone ages, we simply make mention of those capabilities which are essential for the promotion of civilization, and which in their free operation, they contribute to the uplift of mankind at large. The successive ages of oppression and an existence of actual bondage, accompanied with perpetual fear, to be sure, closed the passage of progress to the Assyrian people, and they inevitably ushered in a long period of deterioration and comparative illiteracy, of which we are most sensitively conscious, and yet in the midst of Islam's perpetual fire, the ratio of such illiteracy among the Assyrians has always been kept many degrees lower than among their ruling masters. History shows that either during the regime of the Persians, or of the Tartars, or of the Califs, or of the Turks, the Assyrians became the eyes and the brain of the powers that

22. Source: *Izgedda – Assyrian American Courier*, Vol. 5, No. 6, November 12 1919, p. 3. (*Editor*)

ruled over them. At the present time, the sons of Assyria hold most responsible positions in the various departments of the governments of which they are subjects.

The memories of Urfa, and of Nisibin, and of Ctesiphon, and of Babylon, have always lingered in the minds of every succeeding generation; while in this day of new opportunity, those memories have already given to the people a fresh inspiration and a united determination to rebuild the ruined structures of their old institutions and to resume the initiative they once had in enlightening the peoples and the races with whom they are destined to come in contact. The Assyrians are still the same people of whose heroism and achievements when Gibbon writes, he does so with a trembling pen and with an admiration that becomes an inspiration even to a skeptical historian. Thus, providentially endowed with spiritual gifts and attainments, and as the faithful custodians of the earliest Christianity, the Assyrian people are destined to play once more the old apostolic roll and become a blessing even to their former enemies.

Educational Preparation. Unconscious of the events, the impending aspect of which was surely concealed from the knowledge of man, guided, nevertheless, by a gracious providence, the Assyrians, as if in the possession of a prophetic vision, have for the last 25 to 30 years taken advantage of the opportunities presented to them by the educational institutions of both America and Europe and have developed talents for an Assyrian national university which has long been in contemplation. The spirit of the great Assyrian educators is still alive, and the Assyrians throughout the world are prepared to establish their own national schools, the doors of which will be thrown open to every tribe and race that may be found living in their midst.

The Industrial Possibilities. In the line of industry, although crushed by injustice and robbed by tyranny, the Assyrians have always excelled over their persecuting enemies.

The greatest part of the new Russian Caucasian Railway, which runs from Tiflis to the Persian frontier, was built by Assyrian engineers and Assyrian skill.

Wherever and whenever they have found themselves in the possession of equal rights, the Assyrians have become contractors of renoun, as in Russia and in America. The foundation of a new and a most prospertous city in the United States was laid by Assyrian hands and Assyrian contractors.

Agriculture has always been a speciality of the Assyrian people. But they have specialized in the new development of scientific agriculture, and a movement is already in motion to introduce modern tools and modern methods for the awakening of the fertile soil of Assyria from its long lingering slumber.

Manufacture. Whether it be silk or cotton or wool, the Assyrian mechanics and weavers are prepared to plant and to run Assyrian factories.

The Assyrians may need foreign capital, but they certainly do not need foreign skill for the development of mineral resources.

Commerce. In the line of commerce, the Assyrians made such strides as to arouse the jealousy of their enemies both in Turkey and in Persia. In the centres where the Assyrians are found, both import and export business have gradually been passing into their hands. Undoubtedly, this their success has indirectly been responsible for a hatred that has now poured the vengeance of their persecutors upon them.

Such are the capabilities of a people who ask for justice, and in the name and in the interests of justice, they ask to be created into a state under a mandatory power. The wishes of the Assyrians in America are naturally for the United States, while those of the patriarch Mar Shimun are for Great Britain. On the question of the mandatory power, however, we voluntarily submit to the judgment and the discretion of the Supreme Council.

CONCLUSION[23]

1. The Assyrians, as a historic people, both in the interests of history and for the perpetuation of that history, should be created into a separate state.

2. Their achievements in the past and their large contribution for the uplift of mankind, both in the educational endeavor and in the spreading of those pacifying influences which are the real backbone of civilization, entitles the Assyrians to a recognition of their claim.

3. A nation that has persisted through centuries of persecution in

23. Source: *Izgedda – Assyrian American Courier*, Vol. 5, No. 7, November 19 1919, p. 3. (*Editor*)

the declaration of her faith and has sacrificed vast numbers of martyrs upon the altar of that faith, finds her greatest right to recognition of her claim in her consciousness of moral and spiritual responsibilities and also in the knowledge of her capability to resume the discharge of those humanitarian and self sacrificing obligations.

4. After the manner of the figure beheld by Moses, the fire of the Assyrian affliction has been terrific, but they have not been consumed. The historic nation has still a remnant left, sufficiently large to be created into a separate state.

5. As a belligerent people who have risked more and sacrificed proportionately more, fighting on the side of the Allies, they are entitled to a realization of their claim for a separate state.

6. As a belligerent people who entered into the war on the side of the Allies, in spite of the alluring enducements offered them by the Turkish Government, the claims of the Assyrians for indemnities and reparations are entitled to the very first consideration. The very plight of their refugees calls for immediate attention.

7. We have the most conclusive proofs to show that the Assyrians were urged by the official representatives of Great Britain, France and Russia, to enter into the war on the side of the Allies, and were induced into a state of belligerency with the most solemn promises of being given a free state. The Assyrians, therefore, having risked the very existence of their nation and having made such appalling sacrifices upon the altar of freedom, demand that these promises of the allied governments should now be honorably redeemed.

8. The outrages perpetrated upon the Persian Assyrians should be indemnified, and they should receive full compensation from the authorities directly responsible for the Assyrians' loss of life and property.

9. In the interest of future peace and tranquility, some plan should be decided whereby Salmas and Urmia, including Targavar and Margavar, where the Assyrian abound, could be exchanged for some other place that would be perfectly satisfactory to the Persian government.

10. The Assyrians demand a state bounded roughly by Tikrit (below Zab) in the south and the Province of Diyarbakir in the north, and by a straight line running parallel with the banks of Euphrates in the west, to the mountains of Armenia in the east.

11. The Assyrians realize that at least for 25 years hence, they will be

incapable of self government, and therefore they desire the supervision of a mandatorial power.

(These claims are in perfect accord with the wishes of Mar Shimun and men of war and the leaders of the Assyrian nation as expressed through the cables transmitted through the Department of State in Washington to the president of the Assyrian National Associations of America.)

JOEL E. WERDA
Pres. Assyrian National Associations of America.
CAP. A. K. YOOSUF M. D.
Representing the Assyrians of America
SHIMON GANJA
LAZAR GEORGE
LAZAR YACOBOFF
Delegates representing Assyrians in Persia, Caucasia and Kurdistan.[24]

24. These claims are also published in Werda, Joel E., *The Flickering Light of Asia or the Assyrian Nation and Church* (First edition published by the author, 1924. Second edition by Assyrian Language and Culture Classes Inc., Chicago, Ill., USA, 1990, pp. 199–220. (*Editor*)

Supplementary Memorandum
Assyro-Chaldean Claims[25]

THE ASSYRIAN NATION, which from immemorial times is dwelling in the region of Mesopotamia and Syria has been for many ages before the Christian era, the seat of civilization and progress.

This nation, like her Christian neighbours, has suffered great losses during the last twenty five to thirty years from the persecution of the late bloodthirsty Sultan of Turkey, and lately from the nefarious young Turkish party against all Christians, included for the sake of convenience, under the name of Armenians.

The deportations and the massacres organised during the World War have wrought in proportion greater destruction of life and property among our national than even among the Armenians. Horrors were perpetrated by the Turks on Assyrians, who destroyed, pillaged and massacred many villages in the district of Urmia, Persia. Turkey Severek, Diyarbakir, Veranshehir, Seert, Nisibin, Mamurat ul-Aziz, Badlis of the Sanjaks of Hakkari, Jezire, Midyat.

The total number of slaughtered Assyrians is reckoned over 250,000. Many churches, monasteries were utterly destroyed, towns and villages ruined, while a great number of Assyrians, women and maidens and small children, were carried off to Turkish, Arabian and Kurdish harem.

Even as late as last June and July 1919, Zakho and Amadia district were plundered and ruined by the Kurds, and the population massacred. In the same time the Christians of Urmia suffered heavily and only four hundred persons of them were saved by American Mission and taken to Tabriz.

As a historical people, as a martyred and belligerent nation, who

25. Source: *The Struggle for a free Assyria: Documents on the Assyro-Chaldean Delegations Political and Diplomatic Efforts, 1920–21, Vol.1.* Tatavla Publishing, 2015, pp. 157–9. (*Editor*)

fought on the side of the Allies for freedom and democracy in spite of the alluring inducements offered by the Turkish Government and by the German agents, the Assyrians cast in their lot with the Allies and on this score the Assyrians presenting their claims for consideration are:

1. Liberation
2. Creation of an Assyrian State under one Mandatory Power
3. Indemnities and reparation

The latest military and political development go to show that Assyro-Chaldeans will be left under two different governments – British and French. The occupation by the French Army of the Province of Diyarbakir and Mardin, where most Assyro-Chaldeans dwell and the British of the rest of Mesopotamia, will cause automatically a dissatisfaction and deep regret as the Assyro-Chaldeans will then come under the jurisdiction of two different governments – two different methods, two different languages endangering their nationality.

This will check their progress and their union as a nation. In our claims presented to the Peace Conference, we have already presented our just cause with convincing evidence. Assyro-Chaldeans do not aspire for an Empire, neither do they demand an absolute independence, but a free state, under one Mandatory Power.

The freedom that Assyro-Chaldeans seek is not for charity but for justice and right. They have fought for them and purchased them by their blood, shed on the battlefields of Kurdistan, Persia, Turkey and France etc.

Assyro-Chaldeans claim for recognition on the strength of political declarations of the Allies spokesman viz: self-determination is to be recognised as a sacred right of mankind.

Some of the Reasons that Justify the Assyro-Chaldean Cause and Their Claims

First: The demand of Assyro-Chaldeans for an independent State or Province will not cause danger to the policy or the governing power, but on the contrary it will strengthen her policy in that region.

Second: The name of Mesopotamia that is simply a Geographical name is not an ethnic entity. So it is not logical to call by this name the people of Mesopotamia.

Third: The name of the Assyro-Chaldean State will cause inflow of all Assyrians in this newly created Assyrian State – the home and the Fatherland of the Assyrians.

Fourth: The increase of the Christian population in this region will be a great help materially and financially to the Mandatory Power, in case of Kurdish uprising against the Mandatory government. Assyro-Chaldeans will fight against the hostile tribes and so protect their homes and their government, as of the Allies, they have proven their loyalty during the War for the cause.

Fifth: During the war, and after the Armistice, Kurds and other tribes have shown their hatred towards foreign powers. They have again massacred Assyro-Chaldeans and in this respect there cannot be any discrimination between Kurds and Turks. The Kurd proved himself just as an efficient tool for the aspirations of an Imperial Germany as did the Turk. The place an enemy element on the same level with the Assyrian who suffered heavily in the allied cause would be a lasting injustice to the Assyro-Chaldean.

Further, Assyrians cannot trust the Islamic element, and in order to free all Assyrians from the repetition of the former barbarities and horrors of massacre and in order to save their position from being exposed to similar perils, the creation of a new Assyrian State is essential under the Protectorate of one Mandatory Power.

Sixth: In a portion of Kurdistan, and near Sinjar, there are Yazidis, numbering 50,000 of the Assyrian blood, and their departure from the Christian Faith is of comparatively recent date. There are similar bodies in other localities, who will return to their original Nation and Faith as soon as a New State is created, free from oppression, and free to speak their mother tongue and educate their children, who have been neglected entirely for many years.

The past glorious history of the Assyrians and Chaldeans shows that they are not dead, and that when given opportunity they can lead again the people into civilization and science. The memories of Urhay and of Nsibin, of Ctesiphon and of Babylon have always lingered in the mind of every succeeding generation.

Assyro-Chaldeans are still the same people as that whose heroism and achievements are destined to play once more the old role in this part of the world.

Said A. Namik
Rustam Najib
Major A. K. Yoosuf M.D. (Rep. of Assyro-Chaldeans in America)

Preface from Actual Church Records as written by Dr. A. K. Yoosuf in 1923[26]

V ERY OFTEN THE Assyrian colony in Worcester has advocated to build a church or buy one, but the conditions have not been so good until lately. The ladies insisted to have a church, and they have promised their help and money for the building of a church. This matter has been brought before the Assyrian community and unanimously voted to have a church.

In one of the meetings, the congregation elected trustees, composed of seven persons to look for a property for a church building. The trustees of the church had some understanding for buying the German church on Chandler Street, but after many months of waiting, we did not succeed in buying that church. After considerable time and energy, the trustees bought a lot on Hawley Street for $1,200 and paid it. The trustees immediately took the matter in hand and ordered the church plans, which were designed by Mr. Hachadoor Demurjian, architect of Worcester.

The names of the trustees: AHARON SAFER, BESHARA PERCH, ALBERT CHAVOOR, CHARLES MANOOG, SR., MRS. MENDOHIE OHAN, MRS. LUCIA DONABED, DR. A. K. YOOSUF.

On June 11, 1923, at a meeting at Mrs. Manoog's house at 111 Chandler Street, the church trustees took into consideration the church plans which were roughly drawn. After a few changes and alterations, they advised the architect to complete the drawings as soon as possible.

On September 17, 1923, at a meeting at the home of Mr. Albert Chavoor at 75 Irving Street, it was decided to begin excavation and to

26. Source: *Fiftieth Anniversary St. Mary's Assyrian Apostolic Church Worcester, Massachusetts, Hogan Campus Center, College of the Holy Cross, October 26, 1974*, p. [5]. (*Editor*)

build the cement walls and to start the work immediately.

On September 24, 1923 at a meeting held in the vestry of All Saint's Church, Mr. Manoog resigned as treasurer and was replaced by Mr. George Hoyen – and Mr. Sahag Perch's name was added to the trustees.

Excavation began in October 1923.

Laying of Cornerstone, August 1925.

Church completed in 1927.

Dedication of Church by His Eminence Archbishop Severios A. Barsom on April 22, 1928.

The church was in use until 1994, when a new and larger church was opened, under the name St. Mary's Assyrian Orthodox Church, at 1 Industrial Drive in Shrewsbury. In December 10, 1998 the church's name was changed to St. Mary's Syrian Orthodox Church, under the influence of bishop Aphrem Karim (now Patriarch). See Donabed, Sargon, Remnants of Heroes: The Assyrian Experience (Assyrian Academic Society Press: Chicago, 2003), p. 82. See also: https://tinyurl.com/y8ofpy6g

——

Newspaper (unknown) article one day prior the church dedication of St. Mary Assyrian Apostolic Church in Worcester, MA. (Courtesy of George and Elsie Donabed Assyrian Collection.) (Editor.)

NEW ST. MARY'S ASSYRIAN APOSTOLIC CHURCH

Edifice at 17 Hawley Street which will be dedicated with colorful ceremonies by Archbishop Severius A. Barsaum, Legate of Patriarch and Archbishop of Lebanon and Syria.

Assyrian Legate Will Dedicate Church Here

Impressive Ceremonies Will Mark Dedication of St. Mary's Assyrian Apostolic Church Tomorrow Morning—Archbishop Severius Barsaum Will Officiate at Pontifical Mass in Colorful Eastern Rite

One of the most impressive ceremonies ever held in Worcester will be celebrated tomorrow when Archbishop Severius A. Barsaum in the gorgeous vestments of the Eastern Church will chant the pontifical high mass at 10.30 a. m. dedicating St. Mary's Assyrian Apostolic Church at 17 Hawley Street. Members of the Assyrian race and faith are expected from Boston, Fitchburg, Providence, Central Falls, R. I., Springfield, New York, West New York, N. J. and New Britain.

Ever since the arrival of the archbishop in this city on Patriots' Day eve, there has been a file of Assyrians to his apartment at the Bancroft from the surrounding cities. Notable among these was the delegation of 20 led by Harry Bedik, leader of the United Assyrian Association from Boston. Other cities which have paid tribute to the next in authority to the patriarch of the Assyrian Church, Mar Ignatius III, are Fitchburg and Springfield.

The archbishop is a colorful figure in his long cardinal red robe and black turban, which at times he substitutes with a hat of deep purple. He also carries at the end of a long gold chain

reading of the scripture, when the heavy plush red curtains over the main aperture of the altar will slowly unfold. The archbishop will be seen in a beautiful robe of figured gold cloth lined with nile green silk, heavy gold chains about his neck and embroidered under-vestments of rare exquisiteness standing erect upon a step of the altar. The altar is mosque-like in structure surmounted by a cross, and overhanging all is a round, golden roof.

The archbishop will be assisted by the pastor of the local church, the Rev. Fr. H. Favlos Samuel, in the capacity of deacon and Elias Sugar as sub-deacon with a host of 40 other assisting deacons. Two of the lay sub-deacons will hold the missal, while His Eminence chants the service. The altar boys will stand in two ranks in front of the altar, while whenever shakes the chains holding the sacred fire, in rhythmic cadence. Then will follow the blessing of the altar and its utensils. The cross will be blessed and the ceremony of dedication will conclude with a procession from the church.

During the archbishop's stay in this city he has been attended constantly by a reception committee composed of

PART II

LETTERS

"

[...] We demand an independent Assyrian state under the mandate of either Great Britain or America. [...]

Abraham K. Yoosuf (pp. 73–74.)

Letter sent by Dr. Yoosuf[27]

Charles Dartley, Secretary.

I hope you have received all my previous letters. I have already written a letter from London regarding my interviews with his Grace the Archbishop of Canterbury, Mr. Riley, and Rev. Heazell.

I have laid down our claims and some of the most fundamental points concerning Assyrian independence – pointing out our rights as a nation, our sufferings, etc. Also emphasized the folly of creating a Kurdish state – which will be nothing but a great menace to the Christian populace. They have all listened to these points and promised to influence the English Foreign Office and the members of the Peace Delegation. The members of the executive committee will realize that the things are not moving so fast here, and many important affairs are not settled as yet; they are all looking for the signing of the Peace Treaty with Germany, which is very doubtful indeed.

We were advised to publish our claims and present it in a printed form. Of course, it will cost a few hundred dollars, but on such an occasion, the expenses are out of the question. I have already suggested this thing before, that if the Kurd is able to present his claim in a printed form, the Assyrians are more able to do it and perhaps better.

I believe I have answered your question as to who will be protectorate or mandate over Assyria. I have already written to you some of the indications that Mesopotamia will be under the mandate of Great Britain, but the question is not alone; we are fighting for another thing – non-creation of a Kurdish state. We demand an independent Assyrian state under the mandate of either

27. Source: *The New Assyria*, Vol. III, No. 33, May 15, 1919, p. 8. Also published in *Izgedda – Assyrian American Courier*, Vol. 4, No. 39, July 2 1919, p. 3. (*Editor*)

Charles S. Dartley. (Courtesy of MARA.)

Great Britain or America. We all, the other delegates also, are fighting against the creation of a Kurdish state. This is not an easy task, however, we believe that the archbishop is not in favor of such an arrangement, and I have written to his grace reminding him of this great question. I have also written to Mr. Riley, and while in London, I suggested organizing a committee under the auspices of his grace, with the name Assyrian Committee. I hope this will produce a good result. While in London, Mr. Shamsie was with me, and naturally I have paid all the expenses. He is a good man, sincere in his feeling, having a great desire of doing something.

Remember me to all the members and write the branches concerning these matters, stating our great fight.

As to the name, you do not have to worry; if we have an independent state, the name will be Assyria, connected with Chaldea. The first important thing is securing INDEPENDENCE.

With best regards,

Yours truly,

(Signed) Dr. A. K. Yoosuf

Here is the Whole
Situation Concerning Delegates[28]

Some letters have arrived here concerning Prof. Yohannan that he has not been sent here as a delegate. That Mr. Werda is not working for the Assyrians of Persia. I can honestly say that Mr. Werda has done more for the Persian Assyrians. From the claim, you may judge that we have given more space to them. The Persian Assyrians do not realize that Persia has been a neutral country and that we cannot have a direct claim from the Tehran Government. We have consulted in this matter and written the claim accordingly. I believe I have written to you the attitude of the British Government toward Persia. So the Persian Assyrians must realize that neither Prof. Yohannan nor anybody else can impress the Peace Conference concerning the relation to the Persian Assyrians. Another thing which I have written to you is that the American Government does not recognize her citizen as a delegate, and I assure you Prof. Yohannan has no influence whatsoever. He has written to the archbishop of Canterbury, in answer receiving a very discouraging letter. The Persian question is a separate question. Assyrians of the world demand a place for them to call it Assyria. Their country. That is the issue. When we send you our claims, then the Persian Assyrians will know that we have not sold Persia to the Persian delegates.

Yesterday afternoon I had an interview with a British delegate, Mr. Forbes Adams, who told me not to be disappointed; Assyrians have been recognized, and surely you will have recognition; you will have something you are looking for after; though there is a Kurdish question, it will amount to nothing.

Best wishes to you all. Remember me to all Assyrians.

Yours truly,

A. K. Yoosuf

28. Source: *Izgedda – Assyrian American Courier*, Vol. 4, No. 44, August 6 1919, p. 3. (*Editor*)

Assyrian National Associations[29]

Charles Dartley, Secretary,
Your letter of June 17 reached me last night, and from its content, it becomes quite apparent that all my letters have not reached you. Why? I do not know. The matter concerning Surma Khanim and Agha Petros etc. I have dealt with in my previous letters. However, I propose to explain the situation perhaps more fully and taking a chance with the censorship that still exists.

You will recall that Dr. Y. and myself wanted our passports visaed so as to go to London first, and you will recall that we were refused and we wondered why! It has become apparent that the British authorities did not wish to have the Assyrians represented at the Peace Conference. They claimed that Mar Shimun had left the situation entirely with the goodwill of the British Government. We have learned also that inasmuch as Mar Shimun had left the matter of the Assyrian freedom with the British Government, Surma nor any other representative did not care to come from Bagdad. I am personally displeasad with this conduct of the patriarch, and yet I must keep silent for it is certain that if the Assyrian freedom is granted, it will be granted only for the sake of the courageous deeds of Mar Shimun's army. Of this fact, we have been reminded again and again.

Furthermore, there has been serious trouble in Bagdad. It appears that while the war was going on, both the British and the French military authorities in Persia urged the Assyrians to fight and promised them absolute independence for doing so. But shortly after, the British went back on their promise and asked the Assyrians to disarm. The Persian Assyrians together with the men of Agha Petros obeyed the order and disarmed, but the noble sons of Tyari gave an ultimatum to the British that they had never laid down

29. Source: *Izgedda – Assyrian American Courier*, Vol. 4, No. 45, August 13 1919, p. 2. (*Editor*)

Surma Khanim D'Bait Mar Shimun. (Courtesy of www.marshimun. com.)

their arms before, and they would never submit to such humiliation now and that they would fight, kill and be killed to the last man before laying down their arms. O, for any army of 100,000 of such brave men! Thus the Assyrians in Bagdad became divided, and it seems this is what the British wanted. That is why no delegates have come from Bagdad, and this is why the British refuse to issue any passports.

But, I assure you that if there is any justice left, we have got the bull by the horns. The facts in our possession are too overwhelming not to the heeded. We are fighting, and we will fight to the end.

The Turkish delegates were dismissed and were not received. Dr. Y. yesterday brought some more good news. He called alone on the British delegates and was told that the Assyrians cause was being considered very seriously. Our fortune seems to be in the hands of the British at present; it now remains to be seen what effect our arguments will have.

The reason for delaying in sending you the copies of our claim was that we intended to add to the copies three tables, as to the numbers of the Assyrians and also showing their losses. Mr. Namik had promised to prepare these, and they are not ready yet. But we are sending you this week some copies, which you ready will send the cigars to us (W. Y.) (But I don't smoke cigars).

We sent you a cable telling you that we are supporting the Caucasian delegates. We have decided to send them back, and we will do so as soon as we receive some money. You should send us not less than $2,000, and you should do so immediately, it seem that they had sufficient funds when they started, but on account of long trips and long delays they spent it all.

Dr. Y. was told yesterday that, in all probability, we will have to stay here for at least another two months.

We both long to get back and long to see you all. This is enough for today; I will write you again.

With regards to all the members of the executive committee, we remain

Lovingly and sincerely yours,

Joel E. Werda

A. K. Yoosuf

⋟

Assyrian National Association[30]

August 2, 1919.

Charles Dartley, Secretary:

The month of August finds us still here, and perhaps we will have to wait through the month of September if so approved by the executive committee. Dr. Y. was thinking of returning to the states. I have persuaded him to stay because after the reading of our claims, we expect to gather views from various sources. Dr. Y. has already received a beautiful letter from London praising our work in the presentation of our claim. This correspondence and the distribution of our printed claims, I have left entirely with Dr. Y. who is attending to the matter very nicely.

I called at the new American Commission where I have some good

30. Source: *Izgedda – Assyrian American Courier*, Vol. 4, No. 49, September 10 1919, p. 3. (*Editor*)

Izgedda – Assyrian American Courier. (Courtesy of MARA.)

friends through whom I am going to keep hammering at Mr. Polk (Under Secretary of state) who is here in the place of Lansing.

I fear my business will be ruined by the time I come back. (I am finishing this letter on account of Mr. Werda is suffering from eczema in his head.) Regardless of our loss of business and our profession, we are willing to remain here until the middle of September or, if necessary, more, as we have already referred to you about the problems of different nationalities and their countries which need attention and adjustment. Turkish questions will come later on. Consequently, we do not know how our question will be dealt with and when.

Priest George Lazar has received a cablegram from Chicago signed by Rev. Davis stating that Mr. Werda has written to America informing that Prof. Yohanan and Dr. Yonan have been cast out from the delegation. The fact is that only Prof. Yohanan has not been accepted, but Dr. Yonan has.

Prof. Yohanan would be accepted if he would fulfill his promise by writing to the *Izgedda* a letter recognizing the Assyrian National Association. He has not done so; naturally he was not accepted as a delegate. Dr. Yoosuf has already written to you about the distribution of our claims. We are well.

J. E. Werda.

A. K. Yoosuf.

Letter to Mar Ignatius[31]

March 18, 1921
92 Austin Street
Worcester, Mass. U.S.A.

His Beatitude
Patriarch of Assyrians
Constantinople.

I have been traveling for the last three months to the West to see our Assyrian brethren in regard to our national affairs. I have come to this conclusion that we are still behind other nations as far as any organization can come.

We have neither money nor men – two greater assets that a nation must possess. We have no common public schools; no higher schools or colleges or even theological schools to bring out good intelligent *rahibs* [priests] and *mutrans* [bishops] to lead our people.

When I see the lacking of these important things, my heart bleeds, and I bend my head before and ask silently "What shall we do?" to improve our conditions. Assyrians have not learned yet the meaning of national sanctity; they have not learned how to sacrifice themselves for the national freedom; they have not learned yet how to give education for our orphans, for charitable works!

It is evident that we alone cannot accomplish these things without the help of American and English sympathizers. The Episcopal churches both in England and in America are ready to help us to bring out into prominence our churches and our education, without interfering with our church and her doctrine.

I bring these suggestions to Your Beatitude for consideration. The Assyrian people must hold a place among other nations, and to accomplish these things, we must work *unselfishly* for the interest of our nation. The clergy of the church must work together with the rest; co-working is the essential part of the nation's education.

31. Source: *Babylon*, Vol. 2, No. 19, April 14, 1921, pp. 6–8. Reprinted in *Nineveh*, Vol. 1, No. 12, December 1, 1927, p. 123. (*Editor*)

Patriarch Elias Shaker III. (Courtesy of MARA.)

We had enough troubles and wrangling of the past, the church and the national societies have worked enough regardless the head of the church, and the head of the church has done the very destructive thing, regardless the nations future. In such a critical time as this, we must not hinder of the work of the nation. Every time Assyrian who has the spirit of the true patriotism cannot be indifferent. So, I am sure Your Beatitude will take notice of this fact.

As I have mentioned before, we have many things to do. Since I became interested in the national affairs, I came to the realization that our weakness in every line. So I am thinking how we can remedy our defects.

    <u>First</u> – We must have a press, a newspaper to bring our people into an understanding. (We will have it soon.)

    <u>Second</u> – We must have workers among our people regardless of sectarianism.

    <u>Third</u> – Among Americans – to make known to them our sufferings or needs, etc.

    <u>Fourth</u> – Creating harmony among our people and among the clergy.

    <u>Fifth</u> – To make greater strives for the support of our poor and orphans, and orphan schools in Adana and elsewhere.

    Your Beatitude occupying a unique position, with a stroke of your pen you can smooth the path which has been so hard

beginning from northeast of Turkey until the boarder of Malabar India.

After laying these matters before Your Beatitude I would like to ask of Your Beatitude to bestow upon me the power, *with a letter of recommendation,* working toward to this end.

I am the president of the *Assyro-Chaldean National Unity of America* and Your Beatitude's letter of recommendation will give me more power to carry on my plan.

Hoping Your Beatitude will answer me favorably I remain asking Your Beatitude's benediction.

Your obedient servant,

Major A. K. Yoosuf

❧

Letter to Rev. Joel E. Werda[32]

Jan 20, 1921
Rev. Joel E. Werda
New York.

My Dear Werda: —
It is better to be a little late than never wishing you a Happy New Year. While I was in New York, I tried to call on you but found you were not at home or in your office.

From my letter, you certainly see that I am at Fresno. I am here for the same mission that you had been here last year. The people of Fresno – I mean our Assyrians – speak of you very nicely and respectfully, and they regret, indeed, your present attitude. In my part I feel very [sorry], you have voted yourself for the national union and her freedom; you have aroused the national feeling among our countrymen; and now you are acting otherwise. It seems to me that a real patriot should stand firm over his conviction and carry on the

32. Source: *Babylon*, Vol. 2, No. 20, April 28, 1921, pp. 4–6. (*Editor*)

ASSYRIAN COAT OF ARM and MOTHER ASSYRIA
Designed By
Assyrian Free Association

Assyrian Coat of Arm and Mother Assyria. (Courtesy of George and Elsie Donabed Assyrian Collection and MARA.)

work in spite of some misunderstanding and personal feeling.

The nation is passing through a critical period; you are now aware about the people around Mosul; you may see the hand of England in this affair.

Why the people should return to Urmia, when the Persian Government is refusing their return; why England is sending them there while England knows the attitude of the Persian Government.

How the people of Mosul can protest against the Assyrians coming back; how England can permit such an action while the mandate over Mosul? I am sure you may see the political [pollution?] in this matter. The [makes?] the Assyrians fight against the Kurds and Arabs, and it leaves the Assyrians in the hand of destiny. They have no homes. Can we not do something? I have proposed to have a mass meeting and protest against such an action.

As long as Assyrians have no homes and there is no prospect for their return to their original homes, why could it not be arranged to send them to Urfa province. One of the best fertile land in Turkey; a place where the Assyrians can establish a government; where there are means of prosperity and freedom. My dearest Werda, if there is a chance for the Assyrians to be free and prosperous they must come to a true understanding.

We must leave aside our personal ambition, our selfishness, our dislikes, our personal feelings toward individuals who are not thinking in our ways.

He is the great man who consideres others' feelings, who thinks well of them. He is the man who works unselfishly of his countrymen, bringing them under the influence of good fellowship. It will never do any good to criticize continually. That is destructive, not reconstructive.

We have a sublime aim – the salvation of our nation. This nation will never succeed if in her [?] exists individual hatred, selfishness and ignorance; shall you, shall I, or others bring ruin to the foundation of the national freedom by acting upon our [?] feelings?

The nation needs all the good men and is inviting them to work in harmony; there are occasions which will bring us face to face against some opposition, but we must see the truth and stand firm and try to make the people understand the truth.

After all, we must sacrifice our personal interest for the sake of our national elevation.

Within a short time, I shall leave for the East, so if you wish to answer me, my address is 90 Austin St., Worcester, Mass. I am glad to know that you have been entertained here loyally and proud that our Assyrian brothers have given due respect to your visit.

With best wishes, I remain

Yours sincerely,

Major A. K. Yoosuf

ॐ

Letter to Rev. J. Naayem[33]

New York March 16 1921

Rev. J. Naayem

Rev. Father

33. Source: *Babylon*, Vol. 2, No. 21, May 12, 1921, pp. 3–4. (*Editor*)

Joseph Naayem in the bedouin disguise in which he escaped from the Turks. Joseph Naayem is the author of the book 'Shall this Nation Die?', New York, 1921. (Courtesy of MARA.)

I have returned to New York from my western trip. I wanted to see you but found out that you are not at that hotel anymore.

My trip to the West convinced me that all the burden rests upon our shoulders; that we must work out our salvation.

I have been told that you have been successful in your work in regard to collecting money for the orphans. As long as you are representing Assyro Chaldean in America, the [money] must go to the Assyro Chaldean Orphans in general without giving to it a sectarian aspect.

You know very well that I have sacrificed my time for the cause of Assyro Chaldean, going here and there preaching this unity in spite of the opposition. As the president of the Assyro-Chaldean National Unity of America, I have the right to ask you to carry the same name and for the same purpose.

I am sure you will realize the justice of my claim, union in everything, in politics as well as financially.

This is not the time for secterianism. This is a national work, separate from the religion.

I hope to see you Reverand Father for the next few days, as I can not stay longer. I must go to Worcester to resume my practice.

Yours respectfully,

A. K. Yoosuf

PART III

TO THE EXECUTIVE
COMMITTEE OF THE A. N. A.

"

I had an interview with
Mr. Toynbee, the head of the
British Delegation. I told him
the Assyrians' demand and
showed to him the boundaries
of the territories we are
demanding. He agreed with me
in all the claims, also asking
a state or a province for an
independent Assyria [...]

Abraham K. Yoosuf (p. 91.)

To the Executive Committee
of the A. N. A.[34]

Gᴇɴᴛʟᴇᴍᴇɴ,

Permit me to bring to the attention of the ex. committee a brief report of my work as a representative of Assyrians in America to the Peace Conference at Paris, France.

After arriving in America from the American Expeditionary Force in France, I was approached by a few gentlemen asking me to go to France to represent the Assyrian cause. Without hesitation, I have accepted the offer thinking that it is my duty to serve my poor nation in such a time when there is a struggle for freedom for every nation. I was under the impression that everything was ready for presenting our case to the Peace Conference – our losses and the number of massacred people – that the committee was in touch with the people in Turkey or in Persia concerning the claims of our nation.

After having a bad experience with the British Consulate as regards visaing our passport for London, we secured the visa of the French consulate and left the city of New York before your president,[35] for Paris on March 8th 1919 (Saturday) on the S. S. "Rotterdam" arriving

34. This report which is written by Dr. Abraham K. Yoosuf was brought from George and Elsie Donabed Assyrian Collection in Massachusetts, USA.

A.N.A. is the abbreviation for Assyrian National Association in America.

In this report the following individuals are mentioned as Assyrian delegates to the Paris Peace Conference:

Joel E. Werda (America); Dr. Abraham K. Yoosuf (America); Said A. Namik (Turkey); Lazar George (Caucasus); Lazar Yacoboff (Caucasus); Shimon Ganja (Caucasus); Dr. Jusie Yonan (Persia); Prof. Abraham Yohannan (Persia); Bishop Aphrem Barsom (1887–1957, Syria); Said Radji (Turkey); Aram Aho Ablahad (Turkey); Rustam Najib (Turkey); Lady Surma D'Bait Mar Shimun (Bakuba, Iraq). (*Editor*)

35. i.e. Joel E. Werda. (*Editor*)

at Havre on March 18th at 11.30 AM. We left Havre for Paris at 6.30 PM and arrived at Paris 1.30 AM on March 19th 1919.

For the first few days, I tried to locate the delegates of the Peace Conference of the Allied Nations. I visited His Excellency Noubar Pacha[36] where I met Mr. Melcolm, who gave me some important information. I also met Armenian delegates from different parts of Turkey. Prof. Hachadoorian who had just arrived from Bakuba informed me that two delegates – General Agha Petros[37] and Lady Surma Mar Shimun[38] – will represent the people of Bakuba in Paris at the Peace Conference.

From now on, my work was to locate the delegates of Allied Nations and see them if possible. It was not an easy task in those days to see them, while everyone was busy. During my interview with Noubar Pacha, His Excellency made the remark of trying to make Armenians and Assyrians a Federal Government, but, of course, I could not answer this question without consulting with others. However, Mr. Melcolm interceding said that the clergy in England were trying to make an Assyrian province, which ended the matter. However, all the Armenian delegates have expressed their sympathy and wished their sister nation, Assyria, was also free from the Turkish yoke.

March 24th 1919
Visited Sir Robert Cecil at the Hotel Astoria – the office of the British delegates. After explaining my mission to him, he told me to see Mr. [Arnold] Toynbee[39] who had charge of the Asiatic questions in Turkey.

March 25th 1919
Visited Mr. J. C. Grews, Secretary of the Peace Conference for the

36. Boghos Noubar (1851–1930), Chairman of the Armenian National Assembly. (*Editor*)

37. Petros Elia of Baz (1880–1932), better known as Agha Petros, Assyrian military leader during World War I. (*Editor*)

38. Lady Surma D'Bait Mar Shimun (1883–1975), sister of the Catholicos Patriarch of the Assyrian Church of the East, Mar Shimun XXI Benyamin (1887–1918). On Lady Surma, see Weibel Yacoub, Claire, *Surma l'Assyro-chaldéenne, 1883–1975: dans la tourmente de Mésopotamie* (Paris: Harmattan, 2007). (*Editor*)

39. Arnold J. Toynbee (1889–1975), delegate to the Paris Peace Conference in 1919. (*Editor*)

American Delegation. He took me to Mr. Leon Domminion who is the head of the Eastern division. After explaining to him my mission, he told me that the American Government would not allow her citizens to represent their native country as a delegate. I immediately wrote a letter to the Secretary, Mr. Crew, on this matter, which he answered saying that I might work as a <u>representative</u> for the Assyrian cause.

March 27th 1919

I had an interview with Mr. Toynbee, the head of the British Delegation. I told him the Assyrians' demand and showed to him the boundaries of the territories we are demanding. He agreed with me in all the claims, also asking a state or a province for an independent Assyria, but he suggested not to define the boundaries as it would be in the hands of the Peace Conference to decide this matter. While I was interviewing the American experts on Asia Turkey, Prof. McGee, Prof. Wiseman and Mr. Montgomery asked me for a preparatory or a preliminary memorandum, so that they would know the Assyrians' claims. I complied with their demand and prepared a short memorandum stating our claims and boundaries under the three headings:

(1) Freedom from Turkish and Persian yoke.

(2) Reparation of Indemnities.

(3) Establishment of an independent Assyrian state under <u>one</u> <u>mandate.</u>

I delivered these preliminary memoranda to the Allied delegates. I entered in this brief memorandum the Assyrian boundaries according to the wishes of American experts.

April 1st 1919

I was informed of the arrival of the delegates of Assyria-Chaldeans at the Hotel Dowers. I hurriedly went there to see them. Really they are fine looking men, influential and intelligent.

April 4th 1919

With our Assyro-Chaldean delegates visiting American delegates, I told them my preliminary work.

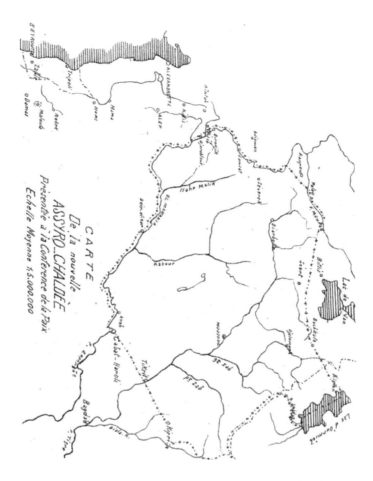

Map in scale 1:5,000,000 of the new Assyro-Chaldea presented at the peace conference. (Courtesy of MARA.)

April 6th 1919 (Sunday)

The Assyro-Chaldean colleagues called upon the president of the A. N. A. at one hotel, where we had some informal talks during which it was asked how much the Assyrians in America could give for the cause of propaganda and also talked about the name – no decision.

April 8th 1919

Had an informal meeting – no president and no secretary. We agreed upon the name of Assyro-Chaldean. At this meeting, our colleagues told us that their interest was for the nation alone and for her freedom – no religious influence had to do with them, it was purely national. That was all. We talked again of propaganda and that Assyrians in America alone cannot dictate in this matter. A little later on Mr. Werda refused to be called Assyro-Chaldean. I have tried to convince him of the necessity of adopting this name, for the sake of unity, which will not hurt our cause. Secondly, I have tried to show him that Assyrians in America alone cannot dictate in this matter, and I do not believe any Catholic influence will enter into this matter. If the British get the mandate, what will the Catholic influence amount to? But our colleagues assured us that their mission is not religious, but for the nation's freedom and liberty.

April 14th 1919
Made an arrangement to see Col. House.

April 21st 1919
Saw Mr. Melcolm with Mr. Werda and after a long conversation he gave us a letter of introduction to Col. Gribbon, who has considerable knowledge about Mesopotamia and Urmia. We asked his advice how to put a claim in our memorandum against Persia and also about boundaries. He, evading the question, told us to write a letter to His Excellency A. T. Willson, Chief Political Office of India.

April 23rd 1919
Mr. Werda and myself visited His Excellency Persian ex Minister of Foreign Affairs. There was considerable talk about the Persian attitude during the war.

April 25th 1919
With Mr. Namik visited Mr. Grey and asked him to give some information with regard to preparing a map in connection with our claims.

April 28th 1919
An informal meeting at the Hotel Powers at 4 PM. Mr. Werda was not present. I tried to make the meeting regular by appointing a president and a secretary, but the full members not being present it was left aside.

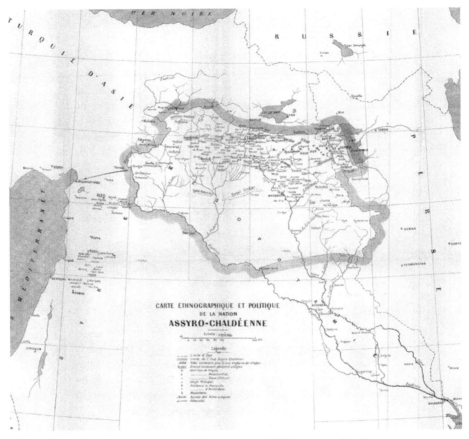

*Map in scale 1:5,000,000 of the new Assyro-Chaldea presented at the
peace conference. Source: Principal Reasons proving the Claims of
the Assyro-Chaldeans to Autonomy in Asia Minor and Showing the
Necessity as well as the Advantages of this Autonomy. (Brochure, 1919).
(Courtesy of MARA.)*

April 30th 1919

I accompanied Mr. Werda and visited Mr. Grey, American expert in
regard to Persia, to know something about Persian and Turkish
boundaries and to ask his advice as to how to prepare the claim.

Mr. Werda is suspicious of the name of Assyro-Chaldean and not
anxious to meet them. He thought of writing a letter to the archbishop
of Canterbury regarding the Assyro-Chaldean name and asking his
influence in this respect when the Assyrians' fate is decided.

This caused the first break of working together. No union, and no harmony.

May 5th 1919

We had a long talk with Mr. Forbes Adams in regard to Mesopotamia. He said he could not say very much then, but very likely the Peace Conference would make an AUTONOMOUS MESOPOTAMIA giving privileges to Christians there. "This is alone a British idea," he said.

After talking of my visit to London with Mr. Werda and our Chaldean brothers, it was decided that I should go to London.

London[40]

May 11th 1919

Left Paris for London. On my way to Boulogne, I had the pleasure and the honor of meeting Mr. Lansing, the Secretary of State, with whom I had a delightful conversation. I told him about the Assyrians – their past and present state; their fight on the side of the Allies and their sufferings. He said "If the time comes, I shall remember the Assyrian cause and will do all I can for your people, but, he added, there is the Kurdish question." I tried to enlighten his mind on this matter explaining the Kurds and their character, etc.

May 13th 1919

(In London) I immediately began to visit some prominent persons who had connection with the Mesopotamia affairs. I had a talk with Sir James Smith, Major Young and with the Hon. Arthur Hertzel at the Indian Office, who listened carefully. He said something about the Kurdish question and also informed me that Mar Shimun had already forwarded the claims of his people asking British protection. Surely, he said, the Assyrian question will come before the Peace Conference, and they will decide the best thing for the Assyrians. I brought to his attention Urmia's sufferings, and her claims for indemnity. In answer, he said "Persia is a neutral country, and we can neither consider it at the Peace Conference nor fix the indemnities," but, he said, "the Allied Government and particularly the British

40. Handwritten. (*Editor*)

Government has made some arrangement with the Persian Government for the payment of indemnities."

With Mr. Said Shamsie, I visited Assyrian friend, Mr. Athalston Riley, and thanked him for his sympathy toward Assyrians. Of course, he said he would do all he could to help the Assyrian cause. I asked him to organize a committee for Assyro-Chaldean, to which he promised to do his best.

I visited the archbishop of Canterbury. In his absence, I had a talk with his private secretary who wrote down all my sayings. I told him that it was a national question and not a sectarian affair. ALL ASSYRIA DEMANDING FREEDOM.

I called upon Rev. Heazell at Crayton with Mr. Shamsie. He has been to Urmia – Joulemerg Hikiary. He knew the Assyrians well and spoke about them very sincerely. I told him the wish of all the Assyrians, which was for freedom and the establishment of an independent state under one power. He has some influence at the Foreign Office.

What I gathered from the conversations I had with these gentlemen was the recognition of the Kurdish element.

Said Shamsie. (Courtesy of MARA.)

Paris[41]

May 28th 1920 [1919]
(Paris) I suggested that we divide the Mesopotamia into different districts, showing in each district our majority, e.g. Diyarbakir, Mosul, Urmia and Euphrates.

June 4th 1920 [1919]
Wrote a letter to the archbishop of Canterbury reminding him of our just and right cause and of His Grace's influence of speech in the House of Lords in regard to the Assyrians.

June 12th 1920 [1919]
There is more talk about the Kurdish question.

Hamdy Bey and Sherif Pacha[42] are here for the Kurdish Cause.

The name Assyro-Chaldean was again brought up. It seems to me that our Jacobite brothers accepted this name in the beginning at <u>Constantinople</u>. "It is a pitiful thing indeed," said one of the delegates "that you think this is a religious movement." I said emphatically "No."

June 11th 1919
I met the delegates from Caucasia and Urmia – Priest Lazar George, Lazar Yacoboff, Shimon Geuge [Ganja] and Dr. *Jusie*[43] Yonan.

June 16th 1919
I arranged a meeting for all the delegates to be present at Hotel Powers. Mr. Werda was not present. At this meeting, Prof. Yohannan spoke about Urmia. I told, at the meeting, of our doings in regard to Assyria's freedom and also said that we were preparing a memorandum which I hoped would be satisfactory to all the delegates.

To make the meetings regular, I proposed to form a real organization, with a president, secretary and treasurer, but no one seconded my motion, and everybody said "What is the difference?" We are all without an organization or without a bureau. On such an occasion every one will call upon the members of the Peace Conference

41. *Ibid.*

42. General Sherif Pacha was a member of the Kurdish delegation. (*Editor*)

43. Handwritten. (*Editor*)

telling them they are Delegates and presenting something different than the others. This is surely a folly and worse, it is an insane idea and not a business way. I made a motion that Assyro-Chaldean delegates have a place, which shall be recognized by the <u>Peace Conference</u> and by Allied Governments. I did not succeed in doing so as we could not decide who was the legitimate delegate. A case happened in recognizing Prof. Yohannan. How could we refuse to let him attend the meeting when all the others had not shown their credentials, and to whom will they show their credentials and who are they representing?

June 18th 1919

We tried to have a meeting again this morning (9.45 AM). There were not many present.

June 20–21 1919

Two informal meetings at the Hotel Powers when Dr. *Jesie*[44] Yonan read some part of his prepared documents relating to the Assyrians' acceptance of the written promises of the Allied representatives to join the armies of the Allied Governments.

June 23rd 1919

All the delegates were present at the Hotel Powers. Dr. Yonan again spoke against the attitude of the British Government. He said he had proofs that the British had forced Mar Shimun and Malek Hooshaba to abide with the English decision – there was a unanimous belief that Mar Shimun and Malek Hooshaba cannot decide the destiny of their people. I had proposed for an immediate action, but to be able to present such an urgent matter, it ought to go through our official body, *which we did not have.*[45]

June 25th 1919

Prof. Yohannan, at today's meeting at the Hotel Powers (8 PM), prepared a petition to present to the Peace Conference in regard to the Assyrians in Persia, but Mr. Namik and myself objected to this. The petition was in the line of returning of the Assyrians of Bakuba. *We*

44. *Ibid.*

45. *Ibid.*

argued that this is not the time for them to return to their homes, because of the present dangerous situation, /.../ the attitude of the Kurds.[46]

June 29th 1919

A meeting at the Hotel Powers (9 P M) at which Mr. Werda was not present. Dr. Yonan prepared an appeal for immediate help to those suffering Assyrians in Persia and Caucasia. I was authorized to see the president of the Relief Committee in the Near East and the American Red Cross and other places, if necessary, presenting to them the real need of those Assyrians in those parts who were destitute and without help.

For the relief work, I called upon Major Carbin and Col. R. E. *Olds*[47] of the Red Cross. From there, I went to see Col. Payson, and he told me that the American Red Cross had turned the work in that section over to the Near East Relief Committee. I then saw Mr. Hoover and Mr. Morgenthau,[48] and they both told me that, though things were in a very bad form, they believed that within a short time everything would be in a better condition, and that the Relief Committee would be able to look after the Assyrians.

Mr. Morgenthau promised to consult Mr. Hoover today regarding my request and arrange the matters.

July 2nd 1919

I had an interview with Mr. Forbes Adams, one of the British delegates, who expressed sympathy towards the Assyrians and emphasized the fact that the British Government realized its responsibility and that, if America took the mandate of Armenia, they would gladly take the mandate of the whole of Mesopotamia.

July 3rd 1919

Received a cable from America asking me why Mar Shimun and others could not come to Paris. *Have sent them telegrams.*[49]

46. *Ibid.*

47. *Ibid.*

48. Henry Morgenthau, Sr. (1856–1946); most famous as the American ambassador to the Ottoman Empire during the First World War. As ambassador to the Ottoman Empire, Morgenthau has come to be identified as the most prominent American to speak out against the Armenian Genocide. (*Editor*)

49. Handwritten. (*Editor*)

July 11th 1919

Expecting delegates. There was some trouble over the signing of our claims. On account of the disagreement concerning the name, we were, naturally, working separately and, in consequence, I could not receive the statistics, and the map from our colleagues as they were using it themselves.

Our Chaldean delegates, thinking that the Turkish question will not come within at least few months time, have left for Constantinople and will return to Paris later on.

July 21st 1919 (Monday)

Our published claims are ready this morning, and I received a letter from Mr. *Ganja*[50] in the Assyrian language, after its publication delayed as it required approving and signing by all the seven delegates including Prof. Yohannan. There was some difficulty, but I undertook the change if they could agree. Dr. Jusie Yonan and Mr. George objected about the numbers and the exaggerated statements as "laying down the foundations of universities and schools and national treasury" etc. To this last question, I answered that it was not a question of how much money the treasury has at present. I tried to bring these gentlemen to some understanding with Mr. Werda, but the terrible personal dislikes were playing such a great roll that it was injuring the national cause. The Presbyterian question was again brought out; really this and other unimportant questions have no room in a national crises like this.

I offered to accept their suggestions in regard to some points, and I asked them for consideration in regard to their supplementary note which they were to present to the Peace Conference:

(1) That they should not send it.

(2) If they did send it, it must be in accordance with our demand for the claims.

In this respect, Prof. Yohannan agreed to write a letter for the recognition of the A. N. A., and we agreed to sign their supplementary memorandum if they would sign ours. I even took the responsibility (rather "precaution") of making rubber stamps for their names.

After reading the memorandum of Dr. Jusie Yonan and Prof. Yohannan, Mr. Werda refused to sign it. I could not see any harm in

50. *Ibid.*

signing the memorandum of the gentlemen as it dealt merely with an appeal for the need of Persian Assyrians. The same nature of memorandum was also given to the Peace Conference by Mr. Lazar Yacoboff for the immediate relief of Caucasian Assyrians.

July 21st 1919 (4 PM)

At Dr. Jusie's room – not all present. Neither Mr. Werda. I tried to arrange another meeting for July 22nd again at Dr. Yonan's room at Rue Londers. Present – Prof. Yohannan, Dr. Yonan, Mr. Ganja and myself. In this meeting, I proposed to create a union between the Urmia gentlemen to work in unison for the sake of national prosperity and freedom. I proposed also to arrange a Committee for the relief work for the suffering people in different regions and, if possible, to choose someone familiar with the conditions in Urmia, Salmas, of our fight etc. to lecture in England and in America. They all agreed upon this, but no action took place on account of both parties refusing to sign alternately the memoranda without change.

July 27th 1919

Sunday meeting in London Palace Hotel. Present – Dr. Jusie Yonan, Prof. Yohannan, Mr. Ganja and Priest Lazar George. Prof. Yohannan read the special news from the American State Department about the latest massacres of Urmia. We thought to bring such important incidents to the attention of the public, but for this, we must have a publicity bureau. The Urmian delegates brought out the question of the protectorate for Persian <u>Assyrians.</u> After considering the pros and cons, I suggested that, Urmia being a neutral country, we could not ask, from the Peace Conference, direct protection, but we might ask for a way to be provided which would influence the Persian Government to look after the Assyrians, or ask the British Government to use her influence for those Assyrians until these pending questions were finally settled *by the Peace Conference.*[51]

Priest George received a cable from Chicago asking him if Dr. Yonan and Prof. Yohannan had been sent out from the meeting of Assyrian delegates and whether Priest Lazar George had joined Mr. Werda. We suggested that he answer this cable in the negative and say that they were delegates.

51. *Ibid.*

"It seems to me that there are very foolish things in circulation among the Assyrians in America."

Our Urmian delegates were anxious that the emmigrants in Bakuba and in Russia were sent to their respective places and homes. In reference to this matter, I approached the British member of the Peace Conference for advice. He told me that it was not the time to send them to their homes as things were not settled, and there was more danger. The very same thing was discussed at one of our meetings, and Mr. Namik's suggestion to leave the matter to the judgment of the British Government was unanimously accepted.

July 28th 1919

I delivered our claims personally to all the Allied delegates and to the secretary of the Peace Conference; and sent others to the London Foreign and Indian Offices, archbishop of Canterbury and many other places including America.

All eyes in American are looking here for a light. Every heart is throbbing for news of Assyrian-Chaldean freedom. I would like to send a message of good news, but I am not in a position to tell anything definite. I will keep up my conversative views and not dope my people with imagination. I have seen Mr. White, the president of American delegates and also Sir Craw, the secretary of the British delegates. Both spoke with hope of Christian deliverance.

August 1st 1919 (Saturday)

While I was on my way to see the American delegate and the expert on Persia, I met Prof. Yohannan who was waiting for Dr. Yonan. We all went together to see Mr. Grey. Of course, the whole topic was Persian Assyrians and their sufferings.

Dr. Yonan asked Mr. Grey why the Allies could not send a few thousand soldiers to protect them. Mr. Grey answering, said that no government would send soldiers there, adding that all the Assyrians did not go to Mesopotamia. I had an interview with Gen. Patin who referred us to Mr. Balfour. It is evident that the southern part of Mesopotamia will be under British control.

I received a letter from the Assyrian Five[52] advising me to go to

52. i.e. *The Assyrian Five Association of Boston*, established on May 5, 1917. *Babylon* was a semimonthly periodical and the official organ of the Assyrian Five Association

THE FIRST ANNUAL MEMBERS OUTING OF THE ASSYRIAN FIVE ASSOCIATION - BOSTON JULY 25 1920

"The First Annual Members Outing of the Assyrian Five Association,
Boston, July 25, 1920."
Upper row from left: Peter Safer, Gasper Dasso, Eddie Kander,
(unknown), Albert Safer, Charlie Chavoor, Thomas Elbag, Barsam
Dasso, George Hoyen, Safer Safer, George Safer, Dick Safer, John
Chatelbash, Nishan Hoyen, David Eskander, Youhanna Chatelbash.
(Courtesy of Virginia Safer and MARA.)

of Boston, MA. The editors were John Chatalbash and Naum S. G. Beshrov. It was
mainly published in Armenian (using Armenian script), but some articles and texts
included are in Ottoman Turkish (using Syriac script), Syriac and English. It was
printed by "Babylon" Publishers, 475 Shawmut Ave., Boston Mass. Modern Assyrian
Research Archive (MARA) has 55 issues published from August 1919 to August 1921.
They all are from the Virginia Safer Collection. It is not known if the publication
continued after August 1921.

Dr. A. K. Yoosuf was also part of the Assyrian Five Association; some of his letters
are published in Babylon. For more information on this association and its publication,
see Donabed, Sargon, *Remnants of Heroes, The Assyrian Experience* (Assyrian Academic
Society Press: Chicago, 2003), pp. 83, 85; Donabed, Sargon, *Neither "Syriac-speaking"*

Constantinople to end the difficulties. I answered that I would not be able to go without the permission of the ex. committee.

August 5th 1919

I visited Mr. Vansittart, British delegate expert on the Turkish question and told him of our claims and sufferings. He spoke very nicely about Assyro-Chaldeans assuring me that the Peace Conference would take the Assyro-Chaldean question into consideration. During this time, there were massacres *in Jeziré*.[53] I told him that it was the duty of the English Government to protect them as she had the power and the influence. If she has insufficient soldiers, then why not arm the natives, train them and give them ammunition and arms to protect themselves, as such things as massacres will happen until the country is settled. He said it was a good idea and asked me to put it into writing. He said it would be a good idea to talk about this matter with Mr. *Buclior*,[54] the American expert. Mr. *Buclior*[55] did not approve the idea thinking that:

(1) It would be difficult to transport *ammunition and guns.*[56]

(2) It would arouse the hatred of the surrounding Kurdish tribes, and they would massacre the remaining Assyrians.[57]

Seeing that the Turkish question would not come within a short time and realizing also the financial situation in America, I thought with a true feeling that one man was enough here, and I suggested this to the executive committee.

I had heard many unpleasant things reported from Paris to the committee. It is too bad that things have not been reported to the people in their true light. After all my endeavors, I am deeply sorry that I was not able to bring the Urmian people together, as there was always some unpleasant remarks about each other. Surely, I thought,

nor *"Syrian Orthodox Christians": Harput Assyrians in the United States as a Model for Ethnic Self-Categorization and Expression.* n.d. p. 368; Akopian, Arman, *"Babylon" an Armenian-language Syriac Periodical: Some Remarks on Milieu, Structure and Language,* Journal of the Canadian Society for Syriac Studies 10 (2010). (*Editor*)

53. Handwritten. (*Editor*)

54. *Ibid.*

55. *Ibid.*

56. *Ibid.*

57. *Ibid.*

our Nestorian brothers know each other very well, so I left the matter to take its course.

August 12th 1920 [1919]

I had another interview with Mr. Vansittart. I asked him if the Assyrian question would come before the Peace Conference. He answered, "Yes," but not as the Armenian question; the Assyrian Question will be settled between the two governments; most probably Assyro-Chaldean will have some kind of autonomy. Surely both the governments acknowledge the services your people have rendered during the war. In regard to Diyarbakir and Mardin, I expressed my feeling strongly and also proved that in that region the majority are Assyro-Chaldeans. We are not asking either for charity or a favor but our rights.

Correspondence with the archbishop of Canterbury and with Rev. Heazell of Croyden, *England.*[58]

September 11th–15th [1919]

There are some contradictory statements and disputes going on between Priest Lazar George, Mr. Ganja and Mr. Werda; the conversation being in Assyrian, I was not able to understand. Some letters also passed between Mr. Werda and Priest Lazar George and Mr. Ganja.

September 15th 1919

Visited the British Prime Minister where I found Mr. Churchill and Col. Gribbon. I had a long talk with the secretary of the Prime Minister, Mr. Philip Kerr. After a great deal of talk about our situation, our claims, boundaries etc., I asked what I should write to my people. "Write just what our conversation has been." I have already written this conversation to the ex. committee under the date of September 15th 1919.

I paid Priest Lazar and Mr. Ganja some amount for their journey and also Lazar Yacoboff.

During this period, I was corresponding with the national council at Constantinople. The trouble between the patriarch[59] and the council is known to the committee.

58. *Ibid.*

59. i.e. Patriarch Elias Shaker III (1867–1932), of the Assyrian Apostolic Church. (*Editor*)

SEIL NATIONAL ASSYRO-CHALDÉEN

CONSTANTINOPLE

Constantinople le 30/12/18.

The letterhead for the Assyro-Chaldean National Council in Constantinople. (Courtesy of MARA.)

October 12th 1919

Mr. Namik is back from Constantinople, and I had a talk with him in regard to the affairs at Constantinople.

There is news of the patriarch[60] coming to Paris, but no news from Constantinople.

October 27th 1919

I expect the arrival of Siverious Mutran[61] Aphrem Barsom in Paris. On every occasion, I had interviews with different individuals; I found out that they all said complimentary things for Assyro-Chaldeans and promised to do whatever they could. There was talk that the French will occupy Cilicia and upper Mesopotamia as far as Harpoot. I am told by an American delegate, Mr. Grey, that at present there is a universal idea of concerning the mandate of Turkey, but he said of course no one can say what the council will think of tomorrow.

November 5th 1919

I thought of my poor Assyrian nation. They have suffered, they have been massacred and fought with the Allies, but we have no one championing our cause. Jews have money, Armenians have American people and the Armenian English Committee and untiring Noubar Pacha and the Greeks her Venizelos. I feel sorry when I see my inability to perform great things, then, on the other hand, when I notice among Assyrians denominational and personal feelings, my heart bleeds. I wish that I was able to show to the world and to the Allies that the Assyro-Chaldeans are the descendants of a great historic

60. *Ibid.*

61. Arabic for metropolitan. (*Editor*)

nation and still possess the qualities of that great nation, if given freedom and opportunity. For the achievement of such a result, we must have a well organized bureau. Unfortunately, we are lacking good, honest and sacrificing men. Assyrians must unite, casting aside the religious prejudices and join under one national flag.

Bishop Aphrem Barsom. (Courtesy of MARA.)

November 6th 1919

Messrs. Radji and Ablahad are in Paris. I took these gentlemen first to the American delegates. It was asked if the Assyrians speak their own language, and I was asked if I could give them a brief statement concerning Assyrian speaking Assyrians. [I] *gave them the necessary information.*[62]

November 8th 1919

Escorted our delegates to see Mr. Werda. They insisted that all Assyrians must unite regardless of the name. They have accepted the name of Assyro-Chaldean, and they wish to work under that name. Talked of the question of sending some men to different places in Turkey, to have a conference at Constantinople, etc.

62. Handwritten. (*Editor*)

November 10th 1919

Received an answer to my letter from Rev. Heazell regarding the arrival of Lady Surma – writing in the following way – "Lady Surma's arrival is the best thing that could have happened for the Assyrian nation, as she has <u>been sent to England by the British Government</u>. She has already been entreaty with the Foreign Office who listened to her with respect, so you can be comforted that everything that can be done is now being done." Tomorrow I am taking Dr. Yonan and Prof. Yohannan to an interview with the archbishop of Canterbury – F. A. Heazell. Today I have received a letter from Adana, in which the director describes the endeavor of gathering the orphans together who are begging in the streets and opening an orphanage. This is splendid work, and I have recommended its continuance and asked immediate help from the ex. committee.

Severious Mutran Aphrem Barsom, during our conversation, referred to his sorrow that, after promising the patriarch to come to Paris, the people in America, failed in their promise. Though his visit is useful, it depends upon the financial assistance of the A. N. A. I asked the Mutran to call a meeting which he did.[63]

After November 13th 1919

We had a meeting at the Hotel Normandy. Mr. Werda and the *Mutran* exchanged compliments. The *Mutran* wished to know about our work during the past months to which we answered him.

November 16th 1919

The *Mutran,* accompanied by his brother,[64] and myself called upon Mr. Werda. After Severious Barsom's departure, Mr. Werda made a remark on a charge which I cannot forget. He said, "Your letters have done more damage, nearly splitting the association." I leave this matter to the judgment of the ex. committee *and the Assyrians in America.*[65]

At my advice, the *mutran* called a meeting for November 31st 1919. Messrs. Radji and Ablahad were present. Mr. Werda was not present. We talked about united Assyrians, but they said as long as Chaldean brothers have adopted that name, as long as that name has been

63. Crossed out by hand. (*Editor*)

64. i.e. Dr. Abdalla Barsom. (*Editor*)

65. Handwritten. (*Editor*)

recognized officially, it is better to go on working under that name. We talked about establishing a bureau for which I have spoken so often and return to America – about financial aspect taken into consideration. For the present, establish a national paper and try to organize or create a committee in London and in America. Severious *Mutran* Aphrem Barsom promised to prepare an Assyrian history, etc.

November 22nd 1919

With Severious *mutran* Aphrem Barsom, we visited Minister de Instruction Publique et de Bureau Arts, where we saw Mr. Lafferre. The purpose of this visit was to find out if there was a possibility of admitting some Assyrian young students into the university for higher education. He promised to see and arrange the matter with the commission.

November 28th 1919

Visited French Foreign Office – from there to the department of Asia.

November 29th 1919

At the British delegation where I was told about the treaty with the French concerning Mesopotamia's division between the two governments. This gave me the clue of writing a protest in our memorandum.

December 3rd 1919

Visited again department of Asia to see Mr. *Gaub*[66] [if] possible, Mr. Bartilot, Plenipotentiary. Saw his sub-secretary, who gave me the idea of the French occupying the north of Mesopotamia.

December 6th 1919

I had another interview with the British delegate explaining to him the vital issue of the Assyrian claims – that all Mesopotamia must come under one mandate. I have pointed out the necessity of its unity; then I tried to bring out the rightful claim of the Assyrians and the benefit to the mandatory power. Again talking about the people in Bakuba and Urmia about boundaries, etc., Mr. /.../[67] advised me to see Sir Hertzeal if I am in London also others, giving me a letter of

66. Handwritten, difficult to read. (*Editor*)

67. Illegible. (*Editor*)

introduction to Sir Hertzeal. He advised me to be in touch with the French Foreign Affairs as the French Government is interested in the northern part of Mesopotamia. Mr. Said Radji showed me a letter from Constantinople concerning the unfortunate affair between the patriarch and some members of the national council. I made an arrangement with the Metropole in regard to this matter. In this meeting, we decided to send a telegraph to the patriarch and Messrs. Radji and Ablahad to Mr. Lutfi to go see the patriarch as the Metropole and Dr. Yoosuf will telegraph to his beatitude in regard to your matter. I sent a telegram to the patriarch under the date of December 8th 1919 "Stop accusations against the members of the national council for the sake of the nation."

Rep. of Assyrians in America. There are troublemakers in both parties, both among the Chaldeans and Assyrians.

December 18th 1919[68]

68. On this date, the Assyrian National Associations of America held its fourth annual meeting in New Britain, Connecticut to which its president Joel E. Werda returned from Paris and gave the following Paris report:

"When I got to Paris, a sort of a memorandum had already been presented to the Peace Conference by Dr. A. K. Yoosuf. It was the best thing that could have been done under the circumstances.

"Before the final preparation of our claims, Dr. Yoosuf and I consulted the American delegation as well as the British delegation. Later we naturally met other delegations.

While we were in Paris, we learned of an Assyrian committee that had come from Turkey. It was headed by Dr. Zebouni, Mr. Namik, Mr. Najib and others. They showed us the claims they had presented through the French Government. These claims corresponded fully with ours. The only significant difference was the name, which they desired to name as the "Assyro-Chaldea." I opposed this name and presented the name "New Assyria" which was also accepted by the fighting leaders of the Assyrian nation. However, we worked with perfect harmony to secure the independence of our people.

"After the departure of the Zebouni committee, there came Mr. Radji and Mr. Ablahad from Constantinople, who were followed by Severius Aphrem Barsom.

"Prior to this, there had arrived another delegation of three from Tiflis, Caucasia. Mr. Lazar Yacoboff, Mr. Shimon Ganja and Rev. Lazar George came to represent the Assyrians of the former Russian Empire. We were impelled to assist these, our brethren, financially. These, our Caucasian brethren, perfectly approved of our claims

Rev. J. Y. *Naayem*[69] organizing a committee for the relief of Chaldean orphans. Lady Sykes is interested in this committee.

I visited Mr. Kerr, one of the members of the Peace Conference, and he told me the arrangement for Mesopotamia. The French and British zones of influence – evidently dividing the country and the nation into two. I prepared a supplementary memorandum in this regard.

December 21st 1919

With the Metropole, visited His Excellency Noubar Pacha. *Mr. Ablahad with us.*[70]

December 26th 1919

I sent a telegram to the Prime Minister of Great Britain and Lord Curzon, French Foreign Office, signed by Mr. Radji, the Metropole and myself. The telegram read as follows:

> "The Turkish question is near its solution. Assyrian-Chaldeans have suffered under misrule of Turkish Government before the war and during the war. Assyrians have fought for the cause of the Allies. Therefore, we beg for the consideration of Assyrian claims during the discussion of the Turkish question. We demand justice, freedom and reparations for our sufferings and ask an Assyrian free state under one mandatory power."

and they said that such were the wishes of all the Assyrians in former Russia. In addition to our claims, we presented a bill of damages against the Persian Government for 33,000,000 Toomans. The arrival of W. Yohannan from America and Dr. Yonan from Persia who represented a certain ecclesiastical body and who were interested only in Urmia became of no interest to us. We had already claimed Urmia, Salmas and Sooldooz from the Persian Government in payment for the Persian-Assyrian losses.

"Then I received a cable from the executive committee calling me back to the United States, and I began making preparations to return as soon as possible."

Source: *Full Report of the Fourth Annual Convention of the Assyrian National Associations of America held in New Britain, Connecticut December 18, 19 and 20 1919*, pp. 5–6. Joel E. Werda was reelected president, and Dr. A. K. Yoosuf was reelected honorary president. The report can be found on the MARA online archive, www.assyrianarchive.org (*Editor*)

69. Handwritten. (*Editor*)

70. *Ibid.*

December 29th 1919

I received a letter from Adana signed by Isa Savoni [Sawme] in which he informed me of a national organisation including all *Chaldeans*[71] Assyrians. I answered him and encouraged him for such an undertaking.

January 2nd 1920

At first, the Metropole did not wish to sign the supplementary memorandum, but later on, he consented to sign it. After preparing a numerical statistic and a map, I delivered it with the memorandum to Mr. Kerr, secretary to the Prime Minister, Mr. Lloyd George and according to his wish, to other delegates and one to the secretary of the Supreme Council. After talking with Mr. Kerr, he referred me to see Messrs. Adams and <u>Vansittart</u>.

January 13th [3rd] 1920

I saw Mr. Vansittart and talked to him about the future of the Assyrians, the British attitude toward Assyrians, and the /.../[72] intending to do. He repeated the same thing that British Government thinks about Assyrians. She acknowledges her services given to the Allies and especially to England and will surely consider our claims.

January 7th 1920

Money affairs worrying the Metropole. I gave him 50.00 Frs. Mr. Ablahad is not financially fixed asking money. I do not know how I can help all the delegates. I have already informed the committee about Mr. Ablahad and Mr. Yacoboff.

January 9th 1920

Visited again Hotel Campbell, the headquarters of the British Delegation, and saw Col. Gribbon. Mr. Montague the chief of the Indian Office is with the delegates.

January 11th 1920

Passed all Sunday afternoon at Claridges Hotel seeing some of the delegates. I was told by Mr. Kerr that the English and French Governments have come to an understanding in regard to

71. *Ibid.*

72. Illegible. (*Editor*)

Mesopotamia demanding again that the number of Assyro-Chaldeans in the region will be occupied by both governments. Preparing the statistics and the map, I have delivered it to the Secretary of the Prime Minister of Great Britain. He promised to draw the attention of Mr. Lloyd George to the supplementary memorandum and of the statistics (Jan. 13th 1920).

January 13th 1920

Visited Quai D'Orsay – French Foreign Minister's Office. In these days, both French and English delegates were not taking seriously about the Kurdish question. However, he said it was a difficult matter to settle the Turkish question with all its many faces; nevertheless, Assyro-Chaldean's claims are before the Conference. One of the delegates remarked that the whole world fought against German militarism, now the whole world must fight to settle the oriental or eastern question. To carry on the terms of the Treaty, powers must have force and men in Asia. I told them it would be a folly to leave to Turkey the great part of the territories again in her hands. She will never do what she promises to do. Never show the capacity and the inclination to govern the Christians rightly, giving them their freedom. Assyrians refused either to become under Kurdish dominion or under Arab control.

Mr. Vansittart asked me to feel French sentiments in regard to Mesopotamia.

January 14th 1920

All the day I tried to see Mr. Bartilot, the French Plenipotentiary. He is a busy man. The very afternoon I had an interview with Mr. Montague, Secretary of the Indian Office. I had a talk with him expressing my thanks for the interest towards Assyrians. He said the Peace Conference will arrange your affair. I brought to his attention the matter of dividing Mesopotamia between the Governments of France and England. I protested against such precedence, pointing out the disadvantages of such a division in preventing the national union.

I visited Hotel Claridges, where I met Mr. Roberts the head of the direction of the Associated Press in Paris. I had a talk with him in regard to Assyrian claims, and he promised to contribute something to the papers.

January 16th 1920

Today I visited the Editor of the Temps – Mr. Lemougain, and he asked me to write a brief statement and to give it to him, which I did.

January 17th 1920

Visited Quai D'Orsay to see Mr. Bartilot, and I was ushered into the room of Mr. Bergeton. He mentioned the names of our colleagues – Messrs. Namik and Najib and asked me if I was in accord with their claims and if all Assyrians were working together. I answered "Yes." He said, of course, the French Government cannot tell at present the arrangement of the Peace Conference for the present French zone of influence is from Syria until Diyarbakir and the British around Mosul. But I brought to his attention the demand of the Assyro-Chaldeans of one mandate, not dividing the country. He continued and said the French Government would look into the matter and come to an understanding with the British Government.

From this Office, I went direct to the Hotel Campbell, the headquarters of the British delegates, where I met the sub-secretary Mr. G. Garbite with whom I had a long talk about our claims. He began to say that there was no majority of Assyro-Chaldeans in any part of Mesopotamia. I told him of his mistake and showed him that he ought to take each element separately, and then he would find out the many places where the Assyrians are in the majority. Of course, at present you cannot expect a majority after massacres, deportations and immigration. He told me the division among the delegated – the delegates from Urmi want the people to return there. Lady Surma wants her people to their place. Chaldeans under the French, and you wish to have a place, a state or a province for all. Naturally I argued his mistake – as all wishing the freedom of Assyrians around those sections that we are demanding – all the delegates agree on this point. Assyrians do not wish to be divided; <u>the only way to have a national existence we demand one undivided Mesopotamia.</u>

Two American Red Cross officers were visited by the Metropole and myself, Dr. Garwood and Major Bryson. They responded to our demand and heartily wished to help Assyrian poor widows and orphans.

Visited with the Metropole the American Red Cross headquarters to see Col. Olds in this matter and he promised to do all he could. He said he would send an urgent cable to the Junior Red Cross society and hoped to hear a favorable answer.

January 18th 1920
Corresponding with Lady Surma.

January 18th 1920
Visited Chaldean patriarch.[73] His eminence spoke very pathetically, expressing his extreme grief "My son, he said, from Diyarbakir as far as the gate of Mosul and hardly anyone is left." "I presented to the French Government the same identical claims like yours, but I have no hope now that the French Government or the English Government will give us anything." We must work together.[74]

January 19th 1920
Today I was informed that the French will occupy as far as Nisibin and Jeziré, but the exact boundary has not been decided.

January 20th 1920
Visited again the American Red Cross headquarters, Rue de Chevreuse and had a talk with Colonel Olds. Major Bryson and Dr. Garwood were [also] present. Colonel Olds made the following remarks:

Firstly, he wanted to know the approximate amount of the need, the number of the orphans approximately, to which the Metropole answered 1,000 which I believe there are more I added.

Secondly, if the work would not interfere with the governing power.

Thirdly, if the Red Cross would not interfere with the other relief works – Col. Olds said he would send a cable to America in regard to this matter. I thought surely this would help us in both ways. First for our orphans, widows, poor and secondly, that it would be a good medium for the name of Assyrians.

January 21st 1920 (Wednesday)
I had another interview with Mr. Bergeton. He said if the French occupy that territory, the French Government will give you "Autonomy" to govern your own affairs. France will never be an

73. i.e. Patriarch Mar Joseph Emmanuel II Thomas (1852–1947). (*Editor*)

74. Handwritten. (*Editor*)

imperialistic government. Speaking of the reparations, he said the French Government will see to that and help the Assyrians to build up the ruins, build schools etc., and help for necessary things – for example, agricultural implements. The Assyro-Chaldean question has no direct relation with the Turkish question, but of course, it will come before the Conference.

January 27th 1920

Again visited the French Foreign Office. It is the same promise.

January 29th 1920

I was at the office of *Le Temps* and had a talk with the chief editor in the Asiatic Department. He said there is no majority of Assyrians in Mesopotamia – the arguments on both sides were strong and heated; it is evident that *Le Temps* is pro-Turkish. However, I gave him a statistic of my memorandum to study and write something about it. The more I see the things, the more I am convinced of the necessity of establishing a press bureau; but "How?" That is the great question for this alone needs good organization, money and men. I am very very sorry that at the beginning our delegates could not agree to work in harmony at least about such an important thing like this. Newspapers do not care for individuals; all the information and the news must come through the bureau. I am also strongly convinced that for Propaganda work we must have a bureau in London. We should have had it a few years ago, even after the Armistice. I very much regret to bring to the attention of the ex. committee that even in America at the present time there is no Assyrian bureau for publicity.

February 4th 1920

I called again at the American Red Cross headquarters for news from America – have received no news. *So far neither have I received any news from the ex. committee.*[75]

---

75. Crossed out by hand in the original. (*Editor*)

ASSYRO-CHALDEAN DELEGATES TO THE PEACE CONFERENCE—PARIS, (FRANCE)

Standing left to right—Said Radji, Moussa Shukur, Metran Afrem Barsoom, Pierre Pacus, Brother Aram Ablahad.
Sitting left to right—Major A. K. Yoosuf, Rustem Najib, Dr. Jean Zabony, Rev. Joel E. Werda, Said Anthony Namik.

By Assyrian Five Association

"*Assyro-Chaldean Delegates to the Peace Conference – Paris (France).*

Standing left to right: Said Radji, Moussa Shukur, Metran Afrem Barsoom, Pierre Pacus, Brother Aram Ablahad.
Sitting left to right: Major A.K. Yoosuf, Rustem Najib, Dr. Jean Zabony, Rev. Joel E. Werda, Said Anthony Namik. By Assyrian Five Association." *Published in Babylon, Vol. 2, No. 14, February 3, 1921. (Courtesy of Virginia Safer and MARA.)*

London[76]

February 7th 1920

Left Paris for London and arrived at that place at 8:00 P M. Saturday and from there went to the Waldorf Hotel where the Metropole is living.

February 8th 1920

I met Lady Surma at the Waldorf Hotel where I met her formally. On Sunday morning, I was introduced to Dr. Louis Western Gambon, who is a lecturer on tropical medicine. He said he will be glad to lecture on Mesopotamia, Assyria and her possibilities "if you can organize a committee." For this purpose, I had a talk with the Metropole as I hoped to find out the old organization and through them, carry out a propaganda.

February 9th [1920]

I called upon Lady Surma at The Retreat where I asked her about her work, her course in regard to the Assyrian Question. I told her of our claims and demands in not dividing Mesopotamia. We demand the mandate of one power over Assyria whether English or French. Her answer was that she perfectly understood it all but would the powers give us these things. The question is on our part to demand our rights, although its fulfillment depends upon the will of the Peace Conference. If it needs, we all demand directly the mandate of the British Government as Mar Shimun has asked for British protection. I left a copy of the memorandum with her, *assuring that all the Assyrians will be glad if England takes mandate of all the Assyrians.*[77]

January [February] 10th 1920

With the Metropole I visited the Foreign Office in the absence of Lord Curzon and had an interview with Sir Tilly. Sir Tilly was not very well versed on the Near East question, or at least with the Assyrian question. After a great deal of talk, he said that the British Government will not go above Mosul and that we are not sure at present about that part of the country. However, the Peace Conference will look after the Assyrians.

76. Handwritten. (*Editor*)

77. *Ibid.*

سهوم اهوه أنها مصحلهانها محطلهاب حاوممه ,بلكا هومهاأههلا
همد نحلى ح مخه أ.هرممهه ٔ اوبمحجبُلِلسرح
وو محلاواوي اهنصطاعي وو هحلاواوي
حملاهها و ممحنما وابيل

*"Members of the Assyrian Delegation in the Paris Conference. From
right: Said Radji Bey, Constantinople; Major A. K. Yoosuf, America;
Aram Ablahad Bey, Constantinople; By Assyrian Five Association."
Published in Babylon, Boston, 1919–1921, USA. (Courtesy of Virginia
Safer and MARA.)*

February 11th 1920

The Indian Office does not think that England will take the mandate of
Mesopotamia – which means for the Assyrian people – one of the suggestions that why cannot Persia be a mandatory power etc., the idea being
this since the Persian Government is under the influence of the English
she will influence the Assyrians also.[78] *The Assyrians is better solution.*[79]

Lady Surma and Dr. Yonan are not on good terms.

I was informed that the British Government would send the people somewhere near the British boundary in order that the Assyrians
may be protected. I have asked about the Diyarbakir district, and his
answer was in the negative, also Hikiary and Julamerg. I talk under a
great responsibility more now than ever as I am informed that in

78. Crossed out by hand in the original. The last sentence is written by hand.
(*Editor*)

79. Handwritten. (*Editor*)

America the Assyrian colony has the idea that the Assyrians have their freedom and that the only dispute left is that of the boundaries, which will be settled by the Supreme Council. I feel sorry to see our people under such a false impression.

February 12th 1920
At the Indian Office I saw Sir Wallace [?] and learned from this Office and definitely understood that the British will not go beyond Mosul, and they will not be able to take the mandate of Mesopotamia. When I asked what would become of the Assyrians, and the answer was that the Peace Conference would provide some way for your people.

January [February] 13th 1920
In acceptance with my previous arrangement, I accompanied the Metropole to see Mr. Athalston Riley, 2 Kensington Court. Severious *Mutran* Aphrem lead the conversation and thanked him for his sympathy. We immediately plunged into a conversation in regard to the organization of a committee purely for the Assyrians and reminded him of his previous promise. He said he was afraid it would be difficult to organize a committee as there are so many, but he advised us to give a letter to the archbishop of Canterbury in regard to this matter.

February 14th 1920
Received a letter from Dr. Malke in Russia stating the terrible condition of those emmigrante whose number exceeds over 25–30,000 people absolutely in a destitute condition, asking me to do all I can for those people. I have translated the letter, and noted the number of the families in that region of Russia, and sent copies to many people including the Lord Mayer of London and also to many leaders in the Houses of Parliament. I have sent also 300 letters to the members of the Houses of Parliament in regard to the Assyrian question and appealed to them for assistance, also enclosing in the communications the number of the massacred people and told them of the damage to our churches, monasteries, schools etc., I have received letters from the leaders of the House.

February 15th 1920
Visited again Lady Surma and again asked her about her work etc. and

wanted her advice and co-operation in our national cause – she said she was going to do all she could for the Assyrians and is furthering her plans in regard to this work. The more I stay here or *in Europe*[80] the more I am convinced of the absolute necessity of a press bureau for publicity. This is the only means by which we can get near the hearts of the people. *Personal*[81] work has no effect and the newspapers do not take much stock; they only recognize a well-organized bureau. Sorry we have not and cannot have it under such a condition, when every man is working for himself. From the beginning, we should have a body representing our cause and through this channel should go every communication and all information.

[?] wish of Dr. Wigram[82] to see me.

Tried to arrange a meeting for the three of us – Lady Surma, Dr. Yonan and myself, and if possible the Metropole also, but I received no answer whatsoever. Wrote another letter to Lord Hatyer's secretary and another to vice Count James Bryce. In London there is a committee going by the name of the Armenian-British Committee, most of its members are from the Houses of Parliament. How can Assyrians organize such a committee in such a time under such circumstances. How is it possible to present our cause in a forceful way without an organization internal and external when the Assyrians on the other side of the ocean do not realize the political situation in Europe and the value of a great organization. I repeat again the necessity of a publicity bureau!

February 24th 1920

I visited Sir Arthur Hertzel; in my interview I brought out the necessity of the Assyrian union under one mandatory power with necessary arguments. He was thoroughly convinced, but he said the two powers have a secret treaty in regard to the occupation of Mesopotamia. I told him that the secret treaty was during the war time when they did not know the outcome and then the circumstances were different than today. To do this thing, needs concession either by one or the other

80. *Ibid.*

81. *Ibid.*

82. William A. Wigram (1872–1953), English priest of the Church of England and author, notable for his work with and writings on the Assyrian Church of the East. (*Editor*)

Government. In answer, he said my suggestions are correct, and he will bring these points to the attention of his colleague adding do not worry of the outcome. We know about Assyrians much more now than before.

February 26th 1920
At the House of Parliament.

February 27th 1920
I visited with the Metropole French ambassador Mr. Canoon.

February 27th 1920
We had an interview with the *Daily Mail* reporter. [?] and [?] Armenian are here.

The Metropole and myself were invited to the reception of [?] of Armenian given at the Hotel Carlton. There were representatives from every nation and any members of the House of Parliament. It has been a great propaganda for the cause of Armenia, where [?] the [?] terrible massacre at Marash.

February 28th 1920
With the Metropole, I visited the Bishop of London H. G. [?] Winnington Ingerham at Fulham Palace. In reference to our request, he said, but the ecclesiastics have not much influence upon the government as most people think; however, I will try to do all I can for your cause. We shall have a meeting at Lambeth Palace when I will bring your question forward.

March 1st 1920
I visited one of the leading and most influential man in London – Bishop Gore. He was cordial but short in his expression. He cannot do anything for Assyrians. I believe the government will give to the Nestorians some place. /.../[83] His grace had shown interest for Nestorian Assyrians. Secondly, I brought to his attention there are Assyrians from other denominations. Thirdly, it is not justifiable to look after one part of the Assyrians nor the sake of establishing a mission among them. Fourthly, Assyrians in Mesopotamia do not

83. Illegible lines. (*Editor*)

wish the division of that country between two governments. Fifthly, Assyrians demand an independent state under one mandatory power. English or French.

March 3rd 1920

Interview with the *Empire* reporter, who promised to make a Sunday story. The Metropole and myself present.

March 4th 1920

A great mass meeting to protest against Turkey for the latest massacre at Marash. Viscount Lord James Bryce presided. He spoke about the sufferings of all the Christians in Turkey and the latest massacre at Marash denouncing the action of Turkey.

I had the honor to meet Lord Bryce after the meeting and thanked him for championing the cause of suffering of the Armenians and Assyrians. I sent him a letter a few days ago and asked if I could send a list *of Assyrian massacres.*[84]

March 6th 1920

With the Metropole, I visited Lord James Bryce, 3 Buckingham Gate. He was very cordial indeed and interested, knowing everything of Mesopotamia, the geography of Turkey. He sympathized with the Assyro-Chaldeans' sufferings and their fighting for the cause of democracy. He said, "I am sure Turkey will not pass this side of the Taurus Mountains." He promised to help our cause and speak at the Parliament. He acknowledged my letter and said, after personal, I hope you do not expect an answer to your letter.

I was told today by Mr. Barsom that I had received your hundred dollars and kept it for myself. Also, he told me Mr. Werda's statement in my regard to the Metropole that Dr. Yoosuf cannot be trusted. That I am causing the splitting up of the A.N.A. What a terrible accusation. What a mean way of injuring my reputation. The Metropole understands me, and others will.

I have written to America the truth, and I hope the public will understand the truth and judge me accordingly.

84. Handwritten. (*Editor*)

March 8th 1920

A letter to Mr. Asquith enclosing a supplementary memorandum of our damages.

London[85]

March 8th 1920

Mr. Bliss, the treasurer of Armenian Relief Committee, called upon the Metropole on my request. After talking with him regarding the advisability of having a meeting at the Mansion House, he expressed his fear that it would not be successful as they have tried some notable speakers, but all have declined. However, he said, if I come to Victoria Street, the headquarters, we may think it over.

When I saw there was no good will and many objections were being raised, I asked them if the Armenian Relief Fund was exclusively for the Armenians. The answer was only 95 %. Then I asked where the other 5 % went, and he said to other Christians in Turkey. On that ground, I asked if the Assyrians were entitled to that 5 % which was never given to them at any time.

They promised to help the Assyrians, but there is a clause in the laws that all the funds would be distributed by an English agent, but, at present, there is none there, but maybe the American Mission may help them or, I suggested, through the Assyrian patriarch, and the committee.

This matter was left for Mr. Bliss to arrange, and I was obliged to take the initial step and ask them to send immediate help to the Assyrian Orphanage at Adana, and the Committee sent a telegram to Dr. Kennedy to this effect.

March 9th 1920

Messrs. Namik and Najib are in London. <u>Our conversations and the methods of working in London.</u> Firstly, that it will be in the same line as ours – Assyrian-Chaldean without giving a religious aspect for which they answered the very same thing – that this is a national affair – they have nothing to do with the religion, and they detest the idea of church in this vital question. They will secure high officials in order to ask for propaganda work.

85. *Ibid.*

From left: Aram Ablahad (Constantinople); A. K. Yoosuf (America); Said Radji (Constantinople). (Courtesy of Virginia Safer and MARA.)

London[86]

March 9th 1920

At the Church of St. Saviour, Southwark, a mass meeting was held for the Christians in Turkey; the Metropole, Aphrem Barsom, the Armenian patriarch or the Greek archbishop being present, *where the speaker spoke of Assyro-Chaldeans.*[87]

March 10th 1920

Called upon the secretary of Mr. Lloyd George.

86. *Ibid.*
87. *Ibid.*

March 12th 1920

A meeting of Anglican clergymen invited our archbishop also, where there were some explanations in regard to oriental churches.

March 13th 1920

Again called at the Foreign Office to find out something definite about us and was told that the Supreme Council will think of the Assyrians.

March 14th 1920 (Sunday)

There was an open air meeting in the famous Trafalgar Square. The meeting was to protest against letting the Turks stay at Constantinople, against the atrocities committed by Turks towards Christians – passed resolutions – in that meeting Dr. Yonan and myself spoke.

March 16th 1920

I was invited by the Lord Mayer of London to a luncheon at the Mansion House with the Metropole. We were driven in state carriages from the Guild Hall to the Mansion House. /.../[88] Bible House. These incidents and meetings are nothing but propaganda.

While again I visited the House of Parliament and was glad to hear the name of Assyria mentioned in the House of Lords, Lord James Bryce mentioned the Assyrian sacrifices and fighting and asked the government for Assyro-Chaldean rights.

March 17th 1920

Left London for Paris. I am glad to report to the honorable committee that our endeavor in London has been to bring among parliamentary circles and clergy, our existence and our claims and have succeeded more or less.

Paris[89]

March 18th 1920

Received American Red Cross Society expressing their regret that they will not be able to do anything for Assyrians in this section as

88. Illegible. (*Editor*)

89. Handwritten. (*Editor*)

Washington has not consented. However, they promised to do something through the Relief Committee.

March 20th 1920
Visited French Foreign Offices.

March 26th 1920
Gave our respects with the Metropole to the Armenian catholicos from Sis.

March 21st 1920
It will not be out of the way to bring to the attention of the Ex. Committee of Mr. Aram Ablahad. He is here for a long time without money. His complaint has been that finances have tied him down, and he can do nothing. He demands money to go to London. He says the Assyrians in America are obliged to help him. I gave him a sum for his journey to London. It is not a question of what he can accomplish, but the fact that he wants to go, *and he needs money.*[90]

The unfortunate thing again is the individual work, and the fact that he is not known.

March 29th 1920
Accompanied by the Metropole, I visited the Department of Near East or India – Mr. Bergeton repeated the same statement that the French Government will give autonomy to Assyro-Chaldeans. France will treat her people equal regardless of their religious differences.

Diyarbakir and Seert though will be left under the Turkish suzerainty, but French influence will be there.

Mr. Ablahad asked for money from London. Correspondence with Messrs. Namik and Najib in London, also Lady Surma and Dr. Yonan.

April 14th 1920
I visited the Bureau of the Education, and had an interview with Mr. [?] the chief of the Educational Departments in regard to finding some way of educating Assyrians in French universities.

I was referred to Mr. Albert Milharid because he said the admission

90. *Ibid.*

The letterhead for the Assyro-Chaldean National Union of America.
(Courtesy of George and Elsie Donabed Assyrian Collection and MARA.)

question depends upon the financial departments. [?] young men to our institutions."

Received a letter from Mr. Ablahad suggesting that I send a telegram to the president of the League of Nations. I have already told him that I have sent a letter to the president which I read to him and also one to Sir Drummond, the secretary of the League of Nations.

San Remo[91]

April 20th 1920
Left Paris for San Remo to join Messrs. Namik and Najib, arriving there April 20th. Stopped at Hotel Royal where the British prime minister and others were living.

Our work was to see some gentlemen there and make our presence known to the members of the Supreme Council. Our presence is only a moral effect and trying to prove that Assyro-Chaldeans were following their rights and claims. I had a talk with Mr. Vansittart and Mr. Adams informing me that Assyro-Chaldeans will have autonomy – *no free Assyria and no independent state of Assyria nor under mandate.*[92] Of course, our delegates are disappointed. Mr. Campbell, the private secretary of Lord Curzon,

91. *Ibid.*

92. *Ibid.*

told me that today (April 20th) Assyro-Chaldeans were discussed.

I have seen nearly all the American and English reporters and presented to them our delegates. We are told again about autonomy. While talking with Mr. Roberts, the chief of Associated Press, said the Assyro-Chaldean question will be settled between the two governments. Of course, your question is comparatively small but nevertheless it is in the Treaty Act.

Every delegate is hustling. I am here and there to do my last endeavor for the recognition of our cause before the final act in regard to Turkey's treaty. I gave a letter personally to Prime Minister Lloyd George, *with the knowledge of my colleagues.*[93]

Things are winding up, and the delegates are gradually parting.

April 26th 1920

Before leaving Royal Hotel, Mr. Forbes Adams called me in one of the side rooms and told me the decision of the Supreme Council. Diyarbakir, Seert and so forth will be left under the suzerainty of the Sultan – the Assyro-Chaldeans' rights will be protected. Beginning Beridjik, including Urfa, Mardin, Midyat, Jeziré, Nisibin, as far as the boundaries of Persia and from there a line drawn as far as Abul-Kemal will be under French with autonomy. Of course, for a few minutes, I was amazed. I was surprised for such a decision, it was a blow for our existence, but what could I do but protest? English will have from Zako to Mosul etc. A commission will be sent to Constantinople in regard to the establishment of some form of autonomy.

Paris

I left San Remo for Paris after a short stop at Monte Carlo and Nice, arriving Paris on April 30th 1920. I noticed a pamphlet written in French about the massacre of Assyro-Chaldeans and their claims by Pere. M. Kyriakos and Dr. V. Yonan, very similar to the one that was given by our colleagues.

May 3rd and 4th 1920

I visited British delegation to find out the decision of British Government concerning the people of Bakuba. While there,

93. *Ibid.*

Mr. Adams roughly drew the boundaries of the triangle Assyro-Chaldeans' place autonomous, while Assyrians in *Bakuba*[94] will be sent to their place if they wish – most probably between Gawar and Ushan.

May 9th 1920

Trying to protest against the arrangement of the Supreme Council for dividing the country into three or four parts, I had an interview with the editor of the *Loeuvre* in regard to this matter.

May 10th 1920

To my question, Lady Surma answered me as follows: "I do not know anything definite, but I have heard the Supreme Council will send an international commission to Kurdistan."

May 11th 1920

Present at Quai D'Orsay when the allies handed the treaty terms to Turkish delegates. Immediately after the ceremony, I hustled again to the office of Mr. Bergeton. He said "France will have that part of the country and will give autonomy to Diyarbakir, Harpoot, Malatia, Seert though under the Sultan's suzerainty, but it will be under French influence – Kurdistan will have local autonomy" decided by the International Commission. The Nestorian Assyrians probably will be sent to their homes; it is much better for the Assyrians-Chaldeans to increase the population in this region where there is better chance of facilities than in those mountain regions.

May 13th 1920

There is still another project said one of the British delegates. As far as Assyro-Chaldeans are concerned in Mosul, they are safe. The people of Bakuba will go to their place. Of course, it will be another boundary line giving Ushnu to Persia. So the Assyrians will be nominally under Persia, but British influence.

May 18th 1920

I received a letter from Dr. J. Yonan, London. If we all appeal and ask from the British Government the place which British Government has accepted – this is his scheme –

94. *Ibid.*

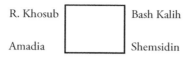

R. Khosub   Bash Kalih

Amadia   Shemsidin

Of course, this is another good scheme, and I have answered his letter, asking him if the British Government would officially give us this place, and under what conditions will she guarantee our safe-guard. Will she be the mandate and how will the people be able to go to that place without homes, without necessary agricultural implements and many other vital questions; before deciding to go there, *we must know the English promise, which money, materials etc.*[95]

Agricultural implements and many other vital questions before deciding to go there. If she is going to send the people of Bakuba then, of course, our asking will not be of any use. This is a good project for our cause in regard to the French Government influence in north of Mesopotamia. No letter from Dr. Yonan or Lady Surma in regard Dr. Yonan's scheme.

May 28th 1920

Mr. Namik and myself visited the French Foreign Office again. We were told the same thing – that France will give Assyro-Chaldeans autonomy. French Government officially will declare this after the signing of the Turkish Treaty and see some of the other matters. Of course, I brought out this scheme of the British. He immediately said: "how can British Government all by herself a place inside of Kurdulan?"[96] adding: "if your people likes to go to the mountain regardless of the advantages."

After all these things, there are two men here – as a delegate Assyrians, who are really a burden upon my shoulders – both have no money and there is no chance for earning money. Mr. Ablahad from Constantinople who claims that Assyrians in America are bound to help him as he has some letters from America, and second, he cannot go to Constantinople; the other, Lazar Yacoboff, whose letters I have sent to the ex. committee. I have helped both as much as I could, and they are still not satisfied and even threatened by Mr. Yacoboff to kill me.

Another thing which your representative was worrying about was

95. *Ibid.*

96. i.e. Kurdistan. (*Editor*)

some letters from America making all kinds of suggestions sometimes with abuses but always complaining why the newspapers did not write about Assyrians. The answer is that the Assyrians have not a press bureau. *No money no propaganda.*[97]

June 3rd 1920

I received a letter from Dr. Yonan in regard to his scheme, who writes me no definitive news from British Government. I answered him again, but up to this day (July [June] 2nd 1920), there was no news.

June 10th 1920

A letter from Lady Surma in which she writes "British Government has repatriated the people of Bakuba to the Vilayet of Mosul – they mean to settle them east of Gawar to Ushnu and give them guns to defend themselves."

June 16th 1920

I sent a letter to Lady Surma concerning a letter from Bakuba published in *Izgedda*[98] – no answer (July [June] 2nd).

June 25th 1920

I wrote a letter to the Internation[al] Red Cross Section addressed to Major W. R. Bereford for the recognition of the Assyro-Chaldean nation.

July 5th 1920

My life is threatened by Mr. Yacoboff, and I am helpless. I have done all I can for him and still he persecutes me. He follows me everywhere I go and [he] watches me outside of my hotel. I have written to the ex.

97. Handwritten. (*Editor*)

98. The *Assyrian American Courier* (*Izgedda*) is one of the oldest Assyrian newspapers published in the United States. Based on the issues in the MARA collection, we can assume that publication began in 1915. The latest issues we have are from the middle of 1920. The paper was published on a weekly basis. Each issue consisted of four tabloid size pages. The third page was generally devoted to advertising and the fourth page often contained material in English. *Izgedda* was published out of New York by Rev. Joel E. Werda who also served as its editor. Werda also published the well known book entitled, *The Flickering Light of Asia or the Assyrian Nation and Church* in 1924. *Izgedda* is a significant source for a very critical period of Assyrian history. (*Editor*)

committee in regard to Yacoboff and Mr. Ablahad – no answer yet. It is a
terrible existence indeed. If I am killed for the nation's welfare I am
satisfied but I do not like to be a victim of a man who has no conscience
and no respect for any person.[99]

July 5th 1920

The Supreme Council has arranged the affairs of Turkey. To solve the
Turkish question, Italy must fight with Greece (which she is unwilling
to do and averse to helping Turkey secretly). British and French will
have to reduce Arabs, then there is some possibility of rest. Even now,
while the Allies are temporarily occupied, difficulties are arising. The
Arab has refused to accept the decision of the European Council.
Turks and Arabs will fight; how and for how long is the question. The
only salvation of Christians and the settlement of the Near East
question should be by the American Government. She has refused to
do it, and the Near East remains exactly as grave and menacing a
problem as ever.

July 6th 1920

A letter from Lady Surma stating that she is not responsible if the
Allies did not give what the Assyrians demanded. She has done all she
could in the circumstances. The power is not in her hands; then she
recites the number of the delegates who have worked independently
from her referring to Dr. Yonan and Mr. Lazar Yacoboff and Chaldeans.

July 15th. –

Our national fate has a great deal to do with the French success in
Syria, and when the Arab question is settled by the French, then it will
facilitate the work of the French army to move up to that part of Mesopotamia, which French Government will be a mandatory power there.

July 24. –

I have visited the Department of Asia and had a talk with His
Excellency Mr. Bergeton who said the things are better in Syria, hope
later on our army will move on further; promising the same thing
again then I asked him if he will give me an official letter for America
to present it to our people, he said yes.

99. Crossed out. (*Editor*)

"Standing left to right: Capt. A.K. Yoosuf, M.D., Secretary to the Metropolitan Mutran Aphrem [Dr. Abdalla Barsom], Rev. Joel E. Werda. Sitting in center: Mutran Aphrem Barsom, who later rose to the throne of the Patriarchate of Antioch, erroneously called Jacobite."

Source: *The Assyrian National Directory in the United States of America For 1960.* Published by The Assyrian National Association, Inc. of Chicago. The Kimball Press, Fair Lawn, New Jersey, p.33.

July 27. –
Visited Mr. Bergeton not there.

July 28. –

On this promise, I visited him again with Mr. Namik; he again repeated his promise, but he said he cannot give that letter immediately for some reasons known to him. He said, however, that *if you are in hurry*[100] to go to America, he will send that letter later on; he entered in to some questions evidently not believing or at least not showing his confidence in the matter of our union, our national union for example he asked have you a national union; like Armenians – ask if there is any Assyro-Chaldean central committee to these questions I have answered in some way that he convinced the existence of some organization, Armenians have one two delegates only etc…

July 28. –

I am sorry to hear unpleasant things about the A. N. A., and the argument of some branches in regard of the president and Rev. Yav-Allah coming to Paris, threatening that if they are not sent to Paris, they will leave the A. N. A.; as far as my personal conviction concerns – it is a poor argument and a poor attitude /…/[101]
"As for working only for Turkish Assyrians."

I beg to differ with those gentlemen, as I will prove that we have considered the whole Assyro-Chaldean affair more carefully, and I have helped Lazar Yacoboff for the last year.

July 28. –

Wrote a letter to Patriarch Elias III regarding Assyro-Chaldean organization and his duty toward that organization to recognize it and help it; a letter to Mr. Radji also. I have answered to Mr. Dartley's suggestion in regards to sending someone from here to America.

August 3. –

I gave a letter to Mr. Bergeton, in regard to his promise; in Mr. Bergeton's absence I gave it to Mr. *Denpere*[102] who promised to look to this matter, as he says he realizes the situation, and inform me.

---

100. Handwritten. (*Editor*)

101. Illegible. (*Editor*)

102. Difficult to read. (*Editor*)

Aug 3. –

Today we had some informal talk among three of us: Messrs. Namik, Ablahad and myself – it was decided to send letters to Constantinople for the union of Assyro-Chaldeans and organize a central committee for a future congress.

Glad to hear the peace between patriarch and national council. I feel satisfied playing my roll in regards to this matter; after all, the patriarch has come to an understanding.

Aug 10. –

After all, the Turkish Treaty was signed – now our question is left with the French Government. I have not received any answer for my letter as yet. I will wait a few days before going to the Department of Asia. I will not keep quiet until I receive a definite official answer.

Aug 12. –

Visited today the Department of Asia. I had a long talk and some hot arguments regarding the Assyro-Chaldean situation and the French attitude toward the recognition of Assyro-Chaldean autonomy.

In reply he said, after having a conference with the chiefs of this bureau, I have decided that it is too early yet to give you such a letter of promise as the treaty has been signed only a few days ago – and it will take some time to settle the affairs there. However, he said "The French mandate is certain and the Government is ready to give everything and every facility for their progress." He argued that there are not many Assyro-Chaldeans there, but in reply, I said to him our massacre until later days and our deportation – the people will return to this place when they are sure of a French mandate and Assyro-Chaldean autonomy. He said it will be given to the people to that promised autonomy, but he cannot give an official letter just now. I asked him when? [He] answered when everything is settled reminding me to present Polish-Soviet Conflict. Repeating again – let your people be sure of a French mandate and of her promise.

Aug. 24 – 1920

I had a talk again with Mr. Bergeton who repeated the promise of the Government, hoping, he said, the French will soon occupy the territory, and settle the things – what you have to do he said – to be ready to occupy this region with your people – when the time comes the French Govern-ment will give all the facilites for transportation. He asked me, where is the best place for the central government in Mardin or Urfa, to which I have answered Urfa – being the ancient capital of Assyrians. The things are better; hope we will soon establish a government like Lebanon.[103]

Aug. 30
American Relief Committee is helping our orphanage of Adana of my many requests /.../[104]

Sept. 1
A letter to Assyrians of Bakuba, of the attitude of the British Govern /.../[105]

Permit me to present to the executive committee the following suggestions, for our national cause:
1. The Assyrian nation as a whole was not ready and prepared to grasp the importance of such a great problem.
2. Lack of a national organization in Turkey or in America founded on sound principles including every element.
3. Lack of a national treasury.
4. Unsuccessfull attempt in presenting Assyrian cause:
(a) having not a recognized body of delegates
(b) no means of extensive work for propaganda in Europe or in America for the cause of our liberty and our sufferings
(c) no unity among the delegates in presenting our claims by a recognized body in a proper way.
5. Lack of establishing an Assyro-Chaldean bureau of publication.
6. Lack of headquarters in Paris.

WHAT WE NEED AT PRESENT AND WHAT WILL BE OUR WORK FOR THE FUTURE
1. A well organized Assyro-Chaldean national union whose purpose will be purely national, no religious or secterianism must enter into this union.
2. The immediate need of a press bureau.

103. Handwritten. (*Editor*)
104. Illegible. (*Editor*)
105. Illegible. (*Editor*)

3. A central Assyro-Chaldean committee somewhere in Turkey…

4. A national treasury for present and future use:

(a) to look after educational work.

(b) to furnish necessary funds for agricultural impliments for homes, etc.

(c) to help the people for establishing business corporation, etc.

(d) for propaganda work.

4. To interest the capitalists in this part of the country.

5. To organize relief work.

6. A newspaper (national organ).

7. If possible, to organize a congress from different parts in Turkey, in Persia, Russia, India, America and in a neutral country like Switzerland.

Sept. 10 – 10.30 AM

Visited Foreign Office once more to give my respects to Mr. Bergeton. He answered me that the French Government will fulfill his promise, that is not very far – as things are going on very well in Asia and Syria. Take the messages to your people that the French Government will give autonomy to Assyro-Chaldeans. He said, within a short time, he will give that authorized letter to Mr. Namik and a copy to you.

Sept. 20 – 1920
Yours respectfully,
Captain A. K. Yoosuf
Rep. of Assyrians in [Paris][106]

---

106. Handwritten. (*Editor*)

PART IV

STATEMENT OF
DR. A. K. YOOSUF

"

[...] It is because of necessity that they want to come here. There is no political reason, especially with the Assyrians. [...]

Abraham K. Yoosuf (p. 152.)

Statement of Dr. A. K. Yoosuf
of Worcester, Mass.[107]

COMMITTEE ON IMMIGRATION AND NATURALIZA-
TION, HOUSE OF REPRESENTATIVES,
Washington, D. C., December 15, 1921.
The committee met, pursuant to adjournment, at 10.30 AM. Hon.
Albert Johnson of Washington (chairman) presiding.

The CHAIRMAN. The committee will be in order. We will hear
Dr. Yoosuf of Worcester, Mass., who desires to make a statement with
reference to certain aliens.

Doctor, give your name, your business, and your residence, please.

Dr. YOOSUF. Dr. A. K. Yoosuf, Worcester, Mass. physician.

The CHAIRMAN. You are a long-time resident of the United
States?

Dr. YOOSUF. I am in America nearly 30 years.

The CHAIRMAN. And were in the Army?

Dr. YOOSUF. I was in the Army until 1917, and I was on the other
side.

The CHAIRMAN. I think I heard you say that you were a member
of the American Legion, Post No. 1, which was formed in Paris?

Dr. YOOSUF. Yes.

The CHAIRMAN. Were you in the Medical Corps?

Dr. YOOSUF. I was in the Medical Corps.

The CHAIRMAN. Will you now state your business to the
committee?

107. *Immigration: Hearings Before The Committee on Immigration and
Naturalization, House of Representatives, Sixty-Seventh Congress, Second Session. Serial
1-B. Conditions Among Migrants in Europe, Operation of Three Percentum Immigration
Act, Monthly Quota Tables, etc.* Washington: Government Printing Office, 1922, pp.
140–146. (*Editor*)

Dr. YOOSUF. Mr. Chairman and gentlemen, I come here for a special purpose to bring before the committee, if it is possible, the condition of some of the aliens, Assyrians, as we call them, that are gathered at present at Constantinople. They left their countries in October of 1920.

Mr. VAILE. They left what country?

Dr. YOOSUF. They left the city of Harpoot.

Mr. VAILE. And where is Harpoot?

Dr. YOOSUF. In Asia Minor. You call it Armenia at present. Unfortunately, they have been detained by the Kamalist Government, who were fighting with the Greek Army, and they kept the Assyrians at Samsun for 11 months. By a great deal of persuasion and effort, they finally arrived at Constantinople, and now they are in the position that they cannot go back to their own country, and they cannot come here.

[The chairman's question is missing.]

Dr. YOOSUF. September 4, 1921.

Mr. SIEGEL. About how many are there?

Dr. YOOSUF. The number is 72, as far as I find, by the names of the individuals.

The CHAIRMAN. Therefore you are personally interested in that one party?

Dr. YOOSUF. I am interested at the present time in that one party.

The CHAIRMAN. You do not know how many similar parties there are?

Dr. YOOSUF. They are Assyrians who are scattered everywhere for the purpose to come to this land of liberty. I am going to speak in a general way about them. This party comes from Harpoot. On account of the terrible deportation that is going on, they are ready to come to this country.

In this connection, I want to direct your attention to one thing, and that is, that the relatives of these Assyrians have been very good citizens. Their relatives are here working, and I believe there is not one single Assyrian that would be a burden upon the American public. They have been good citizens, and, among them, you will never find an anarchist, a socialist, a communist, or even a bolshevist. There is not in the record anything that can prove that they have not been good citizens. As I say, these people have not been a burden upon the community at all. Those who will come to this country have relatives here in America, and those relatives are scattered in America from Boston as far as California, and they will put up the money necessary to secure their people coming to this country.

This of course, is a serious situation facing the immigration committee, but the big question comes up, what shall we do with these people? I know we are overcrowded by aliens in America.

The CHAIRMAN. State that again, Doctor. I do not think I understand you.

Dr. YOOSUF. I say that some claim that so many aliens are coming to this country and do not know what to do with them. To my mind, there is one thing which could be done. You take people coming from Urmia, Persia, who are being deported down to Mosul, may be settled in a farming district in California, through the Government, who will be producers.

Mr. RAKER. But those people are all of the same nationality?

Dr. YOOSUF. They are of the same nationality.

The CHAIRMAN. I am not familiar at all with Asia Minor. All I can get is a limited reading and a little knowledge by looking at the map, and I want to know if you make a distinction between Assyrians and Syrians?

Dr. YOOSUF. The distinction is this: If you say Syria, of course, that means Syria, around the region of Beirut and Lebanon. That is the geographical name of the country of Syria. The other people are sometimes called Syrians or Assyrians, and that is the distinction that I would like to make.

Mr. SIEGEL. Is Beirut under the control of France?

Dr. YOOSUF. Under the French Government; yes.

Mr. CABLE. Isn't Syria a Republic? Don't they elect a president there?

Dr. YOOSUF. No; it is under French mandate. As for the Assyrian Republic at Mesopotamia, it was a newspaper talk – nothing in reality. I wish it was true.

Mr. VAILE. Do I understand Syria is the name for the similar region surrounding Beirut and Lebanon?

Dr. YOOSUF. Yes.

Mr. VAILE. And the country you call Assyria is the larger territory, including that.

Dr. YOOSUF. Yes. There is no present Syria – just like Armenia – there isn't any Armenia. Of course it is on the map, but in actuality there is no Syria any more than there is an Armenia, because the Assyrians during the war fought with the Allies. Very likely you have heard of the mountain of Kurdistan, where they fought with their lives against the Turks, the Kurds, and the Arabs until 1918, when they were obliged to give up because they did not have any ammunition; consequently, they have drifted away from that region to Mosul, in Arabia.

Mr. VAILE. They were driven out in large numbers?

Dr. YOOSUF. Yes.

Mr. VAILE. Thirty thousand at a time?

Dr. YOOSUF. More than that. Unfortunately, there was a massacre. They fought against the Arabs and the Kurds, and now they are down to 30,000.

Mr. SIEGEL. You mean that the total number left is 30,000?

Dr. YOOSUF. Yes; in Mosul.

The CHAIRMAN. Those are the people who you designate as Assyrians?

Dr. YOOSUF. As Assyrians. These people are the same, only they live in the region of Harpoot, among the Armenians.

The CHAIRMAN. So the Armenians are one class without a country, and the Assyrians are another class without a country?

Dr. YOOSUF. Of course, they have not any country at all. They are under the Turkish dominion at present.

The CHAIRMAN. Who is taking care of these particular people in whom you are interested?

Dr. YOOSUF. These people are being taken care of by their own people in America.

The CHAIRMAN. Money is being sent to them?

Dr. YOOSUF. Money is sent to them; yes.

The CHAIRMAN. Sent to them in Constantinople?

Dr. YOOSUF. Sent to them in Constantinople, and they want to send money to them in Harpoot, for them to leave the country and come to America with their families and relatives.

The CHAIRMAN. Have they all families and relatives here?

Dr. YOOSUF. Yes, sir. I have the names and addresses of the people here, where they are living.

The CHAIRMAN. You are referring to those 72, of course.

Dr. YOOSUF. Yes.

Mr SIEGEL. And you are not referring to the 30,000?

Dr. YOOSUF. No; because most of them are not coming here anyway, although a few of them will come. Those are scattered; they are not in Mosul, because Mosul is at present under the dominion of the British Government.

The CHAIRMAN. It is pretty fair to assume that all of those refugee Assyrians who are in Constantinople, who have relatives in the United States, will come to the United States if their relatives can pay their way?

Dr. YOOSUF. Yes, sir. They are willing to pay and to put up a bond for them.

The CHAIRMAN. I am talking about all of them now, and you are referring to the 72.

Dr. YOOSUF. I am speaking for the 72 now. Out of that 72 who could come, the relatives are willing to pay. I do not know whether all of them would come or not, but those who are willing to come are all Assyrians, and their relatives are willing to pay their expenses and to put up a bond for them.

The CHAIRMAN. What do you think the expense would be of bringing one Assyrian from Constantinople to Boston?

Dr. YOOSUF. It depends altogether. If they come first-class, steerage passenger, very likely it would be about $80. That $80 would pay for the ticket.

Mr. SIEGEL. Are you sure that you could bring one of them over here for $80 now?

Dr. YOOSUF. I do not know exactly what the price is; it is fluctuating so much.

The CHAIRMAN. If those people come, don't they have to have passports from some country?

Dr. YOOSUF. Of course, they have to have a passport, and they have to get it from the Turkish Government.

The CHAIRMAN. Have you met any of them who have come from Constantinople?

Dr. YOOSUF. From Constantinople; yes.

Mr. VAILE. The Turkish Government is not particularly friendly to them, is it?

Dr. YOOSUF. No; because they fight against Turks.

Mr. VAILE. They might be willing to give passports in order to get them out of the country.

Dr. YOOSUF. Yes. First they will get all the money and then say, "Go ahead."

The CHAIRMAN. I dislike very much to bring up a discussion on a religious matter, but the Turkish Government opposes these people on the ground of religion, does it not?

Dr. YOOSUF. That is the principal part of it; yes.

The CHAIRMAN. And it opposes the Armenians for the same reason?

Dr. YOOSUF. Yes, sir.

The CHAIRMAN. What is the predominant religion of the people there?

Dr. YOOSUF. Generally speaking, in old Turkey, the majority are Moslems, Mohammedans on account of continual persecution and deportation of the Christians. On account of the deportations for the last five years, in every city, from Asia Minor as far as Aleppo, dominated by the Turks – they are Mohammedans – and on the Mountain of Kurdistan, the same thing applies.

Mr. SIEGEL. If I understood the chairman correctly his question was with reference to these 72 people.

Dr. YOOSUF. Oh, they are Christians, those Assyrians.

The CHAIRMAN. Those people are Christian Assyrians?

Dr. YOOSUF. Yes.

The CHAIRMAN. And your information is that the Armenians are Christian people?

Dr. YOOSUF. Yes. Anybody that comes from Turkey, of course, the American Government will consider him as a Turk. They will ask "Where were you born?" and you will say "In Turkey," and consequently they will say you are a Turk. But, gentlemen, I think dealing with the situation in Turkey that we ought to take the races separately and classify them according to their race.

Mr. VAILE. You say that the Turkish Government discriminates against them and persecutes them perhaps on account of their religion. Now, I do not remember reading about any persecutions of Greeks on account of their Christian religion, or of the Jews by the Turkish people. What is their attitude toward the people of those religions?

Dr. YOOSUF. The Turks have a little different idea toward the Jews. The Jews, of course, are similar in belief; at least, they believe in one God. They do not believe in Christ, but in believing in one God, they are somewhat on the same ground.

146

Another thing, the Jews have never been against the Turkish Government at any time, because they have not been persecuted by the Turks, even though they have not be persecuted, but wanted free, and they have the Palestine.

Mr. VAILE. Isn't that the gist of it, that the Jews and the Greeks have not opposed the Turkish Government?

Dr. YOOSUF. Oh, the Greeks are fighting the Turkish Government now. I do not see how you can make that out as not against the Turks.

Mr. WHITE. You are speaking now of the Greek Catholic Church?

Dr. YOOSUF. The Greek Catholic Church and the Greek Orthodox.

Mr. WHITE. That was the established church of Russia before the overthrow, before the revolution, was it not, the Greek Church?

Dr. YOOSUF. Yes. Centuries ago the Roman Catholic Church was dominating, but after many years, they were separated, and the Armenian and the Assyrian are the only two sister churches now that are separated from the category of the Catholic religion. The Greek Church is a little different from the rest, and the Armenian and Assyrian churches are sister churches, because they believe principally the same thing.

Gentlemen, you will find some information along that line in a little book, which was published by me in 1905, which is in the Congressional Library, which is entitled "The Christian Sufferings Under the Mohammedans," just a little pamphlet that I have endeavored to put before the American public, to show exactly the relations between the Christians and the Turks.

Mr. SIEGEL. The book is published under your name and written by you?

Dr. YOOSUF. Yes, sir.

Mr. RAKER. What church or denomination do these Assyrians that you speak of belong to?

Dr. YOOSUF. The Assyrian Orthodox Church.

Mr. RAKER. That is not connected with the Greek or Catholic church?

Dr. YOOSUF. No.

Mr. RAKER. And it is disconnected with the Jewish church?

Dr. YOOSUF. It has nothing whatever to do with it.

Mr. RAKER. And it is in every way disconnected with the Moslem church?

Dr. YOOSUF. It has nothing at all to do with the Moslem church. The Moslems do not believe in Christianity at all. The Assyrian and

Armenian churches are different from the Mohammedan church and the Jewish church.

The CHAIRMAN. We will not pursue that any further.

I will ask you now to come right down to this situation regarding the 72 people. Have they got tickets to come over to the United States?

Dr. YOOSUF. They have not. There is the difficulty. The American consul will not visé the passports on account of the restrictions.

The CHAIRMAN. On account of the quota being exhausted?

Dr. YOOSUF. Yes.

The CHAIRMAN. Do these people come under the classification of "other Asia?"

Dr. YOOSUF. I do not know how that would be.

Mr. SIEGEL. If I may interrupt, the Turkish and Greek quotas are exhausted for the year.

Mr. WHITE. What has been brought out by the witness. I came in late. Will these 72 referred to in the discussion, will they be identified as coming from Armenia or any other country than Turkey?

Mr. SIEGEL. They might be identified as coming from Syria, but that quota is also closed for the year. If they come from Turkey, that is closed; and "All other Asia" is closed, too.

The CHAIRMAN. They were born in the country -- they were born in Turkey?

Dr. YOOSUF. In Turkey. That is the reason I brought up the fact that because a man comes from Turkey, you will say that he is a Turk. Of course, under that condition, the quota is full, but I believe it is right and just to take the separate races as races there.

Mr. RAKER. Weren't they part of the Turkish Government, born under the Turkish flag?

Dr. YOOSUF. Yes, sir.

Mr. RAKER. And they claim that as their home?

Dr. YOOSUF. Yes.

Mr. RAKER. The only difference is in their religion and in the stock or race?

Dr. YOOSUF. Yes, sir.

The CHAIRMAN. Here is a situation where at the close of the war they were a minority race of Christian people, and they are up against that, up against the fact that they are a minority race, and also up against the religious situation.

Dr. YOOSUF. Yes.

The CHAIRMAN. Isn't it possible that that situation can be straightened out over there, and that those people who are in a country where they have a British protectorate can be saved from persecution?

Dr. YOOSUF. With regard to those in Mosul, of course there is no persecution, but those in Cilicia and upper Asia Minor, they cannot get to Mosul under any circumstances, and it is a question of what they are going to do. They can not get back to Harpoot.

Mr. SIEGEL. How far is that away?

Dr. YOOSUF. With a caravan, it takes 15 days from Samsun to Harpoot.

The CHAIRMAN. Do they cross on animals?

Dr. YOOSUF. Yes, they come by animals – mules and horses. Sometimes they are able to get a carriage.

Mr. RAKER. It cannot be more than a couple of hundred miles from Constantinople.

Dr. YOOSUF. From the Black Sea they come by boat, from Samsun to Constantinople, and it only takes about two days.

Mr. RAKER. Where do they get on the boat, in the Black Sea?

Dr. YOOSUF. At Samsun.

Mr. RAKER. What is the nature of the persecution against them now?

Dr. YOOSUF. The persecution began in 1915 and in 1895. What the difficulty is, I do not know; I cannot tell, but, of course, like any other people, they want to be free from the persecution of the Turks, and they want to be independent, at least they want to be under a rule where they can live safely and without molestation. That is the whole idea. Because they kicked against the Turkish Government, they were persecuted.

Mr. RAKER. Most of those difficulties have been settled. They have got free republics over in Russia and along the western border of Russia, down the border of Germany. Then these Turks have been having their troubles. England and France have been in there. What is the principal persecution of these people now by the Government from which they originally came?

Dr. YOOSUF. The same identical trouble that it was before. The first thing is the idea that Turkey for Turks. They do not want any Christians living there. They are trying to send them away. According to Turks and their belief that the Christians are slaves to the Turks, calling the Christians "Gavour."

Mr. RAKER. I know, but what do they do to them?

Dr. YOOSUF. They massacre them, and then they deport them.

Mr. WHITE. They kill them, do they not?

Dr. YOOSUF. Yes.

Mr. WHITE. They cut their throats?

Dr. YOOSUF. Yes. My nephew was taken from a college and hanged without any court.

Mr. CABLE. Who did that? The Turks?

Dr. YOOSUF. Yes, sir. And I lost my father and my mother.

The CHAIRMAN. Now, to get back to these particular 72 people that you are appearing for, while it will not be necessary to give the names, you can give the cities to which they propose to go, and also the ages of the candidates for admission, if you have it.

Dr. YOOSUF. The first nine are to go to Worcester, Mass.; one to Fresno, Calif.; one to another town in Massachusetts; three or four more going to Massachusetts; five or six going to Lynn, Mass.; one to Providence, RI; one to Watertown, Mass.; three for Naljan, Calif.; three more for Watertown, Mass.; five for Worcester; five for Fitchburg, Mass.; two for New York; two more to Fresno; and eight for Worcester.

The CHAIRMAN. They are coming to their relatives?

Dr. YOOSUF. All of them.

The CHAIRMAN. They have not started yet?

Dr. YOOSUF. No.

The CHAIRMAN. I want to ask you with regard to the condition in Constantinople, your latest information with regard to the refugees there – the number – how they are going to be fed? How many you think will starve to death this winter, and so on.

Dr. YOOSUF. With regard to the refugees in Constantinople, of course, I have limited myself to the 72 that I am interested in at present. Is that what you want, or in general?

The CHAIRMAN. Do you know anything about the general situation in Constantinople?

Dr. YOOSUF. In general the situation is known to you all – the political situation – but as far as the living condition is concerned, living is extremely high and it is very hard to secure the necessary things for living. The relatives of people there are trying to supply the necessary money for their living until there is a chance to bring them to this country.

The CHAIRMAN. Now, those relatives know that other people, not their relatives, will die in Constantinople this year?

Dr. YOOSUF. Yes; most of them.

The CHAIRMAN. A lot of them.

Dr. YOOSUF. I received a letter from Constantinople stating that they are perfectly willing to do anything, but they cannot find work.

The CHAIRMAN. Are more refugees coming into Constantinople all the time?

Dr. YOOSUF. Nearly all the time; yes, sir.

The CHAIRMAN. The British Government there has not succeeded in keeping out the refugees?

Dr. YOOSUF. No.

The CHAIRMAN. Do you know why the American Red Cross has ceased its activities there among the refugees?

Dr. YOOSUF. Well, very likely there is some reason. It is not for me to say.

The CHAIRMAN. What do you think?

Dr. YOOSUF. The reason, I suppose, is this way. The Red Cross do not have sufficient funds as they used to have, and another reason is the Red Cross is not doing any more, because of the Near East work, which is doing the same thing. They do not want to mix the two organizations. Where one is working, the other one is not working.

Mr. RAKER. Now, it is practically true, isn't it, that many of these people in the various countries, ones you refer to, and others, have sought to gain political prominence, that is, on one side or the other, against the established conditions, and when they lose and the other side wins, they feel that they are badly treated and want to get out and get to the United States. Isn't there a good deal of truth in that?

Dr. YOOSUF. You would have to specify what country you mean so that I could answer. So far as Syria is concerned, they have not the two parties at all. If you refer to Armenia, of course, there are. As far as the Assyrians are concerned, they do not have any government at all which they can divide into two classes, absolutely nothing of that kind.

Mr. RAKER. Do you understand that there is no Government in those countries at all?

Dr. YOOSUF. Not at all. It is Turkish Government farther up in the northern part of Asia Minor, which you call Armenia. Of course, that is in the hands of the Bolsheviks, and some of the Armenians were obliged to accept the Bolshevik government.

Mr. RAKER. The Bolsheviks have run what they called their government?

Dr. YOOSUF. Yes.

Mr. RAKER. And the Turks run what they call their government?

Dr. YOOSUF. Yes.

Mr. RAKER. And these people are under these various jurisdictions or sovereignties?

Dr. YOOSUF. Yes.

Mr. RAKER. And they are opposed now to present conditions.

Dr. YOOSUF. It is not a question of opposition.

Mr. RAKER. That is the situation, isn't it?

Dr. YOOSUF. No; it is not a question of opposition. There is no safety in the way they are living. If the Turkish Government to-day would give the necessary protection to life and property, and leave out the persecution of them because they are Christians, they would not want to come here at all. It is because of necessity that they want to come here. There is no political reason, especially with the Assyrians. I am president of the Assyrian and Chaldean National Union in America.

Mr. WHITE. In a single word, there is no general toleration in Turkey of the Christians?

Dr. YOOSUF. No, sir.

Mr. WHITE. But there are no two parties?

Dr. YOOSUF. No, sir.

Mr. WHITE. And there never has been. So far as the question of ascendency is concerned, the Moslems, the Turks, have been, and are now, in the ascendancy.

Dr. YOOSUF. Yes. Turks and musselmen are the same thing – one national name, the other religious, and we say Turk or musselman or Mohammedan are the same.

The CHAIRMAN. The committee thanks you for your statement.

PART V

WRITINGS REGARDING
DR. A. K. YOOSUF

"

[...] they are called
'Assyrian Jacobites,' and
are descendants of the old
Assyrian stock, well known in
history. [...]

Fitchburg Sentinal (p. 152.)

Assyrian Benefit Society Organized[108]

LOCAL ASSYRIANS MET at the National House, Thursday evening, and organized a branch of the Assyrian Benefit Association, an organization formed in Worcester, in July, 1897, through the efforts of Dr. Arthur K. Yoosuf of that city and is in flourishing condition. The Assyrians in Fitchburg number about 50, five families in all, most of them young men, active and intelligent. They are studious and industrious – a very energetic people. They are called "Assyrian Jacobites," and are descendants of the old Assyrian stock, well known in history.

At their meeting Thursday evening, they had as guest of honor, Dr. A. K. Yoosuf, of Worcester, who spoke about the new society its necessity in the little colony and urged the members to support it morally and financially.

After the meeting, Landlord Charles Peters, of the National House, who belongs to an aristocratic family in the old country, served an elegant banquet to the members of the new society and several American guests. This was followed by instrumental music, including Oriental and European compositions.

108. Source: *Fitchburg Sentinal*, 1898. (*Editor*)

Events of the Day[109]

Dr. ARTHUR K. YOOSUF of Worcester, Mass. who volunteered for hospital duty in the Turkish Army and was stationed in Stamboul, says that more than 8,500 sick wounded soldiers passed under his hands.

---

109. Source: *Charlotte Daily Observer*, Friday, September 5 1913, p. 4. (*Editor*)

Yoosuf, Abraham Kevork[110]

Yoosuf, abraham kevork, M.D.; b. Turkey, Asia, Dec. 17,
1867; Kevork and Sarah (Nallband) Yoosuf; A.B., Central Turkey
Coll., 1886; arrived in America, 1889; M. D., Baltimore Med. Coll. (U.
of Med.), 1896. Practiced in Worcester, Mass., since 1896. Mem.
A. M. A., Mass. Med. Soc., Worcester Dist. Med. Soc., Assyrian Soc.
(pres.), Internat. Congress on Tuberculosis, Child Study Congress,
etc. Conglist. Mem. B. P. O. Clubs: Congregational, Twentieth
Century. Author: Religion of Mohammed; Christian Sufferings;
Surgery in Warfare (pamphlet). Visited Europe, 1912, and served as
chief surgeon in hosp., under Turkish Red Crescent Soc.; awarded
medal of Red Crescent So. by sultan of Turkey. Address: 82 Franklin
St., Worcester, Mass.

110. Source: Albert Marquis Nelson, 1916, *Who's Who in New England*, 2nd edition,
Chicago, A W Marquis and Company. (*Editor*)

The Assyrian Colony
in Worcester, Mass.[111]

THE LIMITED SPACE in these pages does not permit us to write in detail concerning our visit to Worcester, Massachusetts. Perhaps it would suffice to say that nowhere has an Assyrian colony given us so much encouragement and inspiration in the performance of our duty toward the unification of the Assyrian Nation as this colony. The picture of that patriotic meeting is still vivid before us, and the remembrances of friends are still refreshing. Here in a town of one of the Eastern States we find the nucleus of the first Assyrian library. Here, in this colony, we found the patriotic women whose womanly hearts are burning with national zeal. Here, in this colony, we found a sample of the possibilities of the Assyrian womanhood in the most able, intelligent and patriotic essays which were read by the Assyrian women. This colony is fortunate, in having in their midst, a group of intelligent leaders, and among these leaders, is our honored friend and brother, Dr. A. Yoosuf, whose sole ambition is the resurrection of the Assyrian Nation. Every Assyrian ought to feel proud of Dr. Yoosuf, who is so well known and respected by all the inhabitants of this American town. The hospitality of the Assyrians in this colony was characteristically Assyrian, and, therefore, it needs no description... EDITOR.

111. Source: *The New Assyria*, Vol. I, No. 7, March 15 1917, pp. 8–9. The editor is Joel E. Werda. (*Editor*)

Assyrian Young Men's Picnic Attended by Lowell Parties – Farewell to Dr. Yoosuf[112]

A NUMBER OF Lowell people attended the annual picnic of the Assyrian Young Men's Association which was held this year in East Watertown a few days ago.

The outing was attended by a large number of people from all over the state, and a very enjoyable program was carried out. Many noted speakers from New York City and New Jersey were present and addressed the assemblage. Among the 25 or so Lowell people who attended were, Mr. and Mrs. George Hoyen, Miss. Y. B. Atlas, C. Atlas, George Atlas and M. A. Hoyen.

Another recent event in Assyrian circles was a farewell reception given to Dr. A. K. Yoosuf of Worcester who has been assigned to the medical corps of the regular army at Ayer. Dr. Yoosuf, who has been given a commission as lieutenant, is well known to local Assyrians. He was stationed at a hospital near Constantinople during the Balkan War.

The reception was given in Worcester several evenings ago and was attended by a number of local people.

112. Source: *The Lowell Sun*, Friday, September 14 1917, p. 2. (*Editor*)

Yank Army must rebuild France[113]

CAPT. A. K. YOOSUF Says Other Troops Too Worn Out.

"The American army is the army that is going to rebuild France," says A. K. Yoosuf, medical corps, who arrived in Worcester last week, after passing several months overseas doing medical work among the wounded American soldiers in England and in France. According to Capt. Yoosuf, the French, British and Belgian armies, although showing wonderful spirit, are too tired out after the four strenuous years they have been thru, to accomplish reconstruction work as well as the Americans can.

The American army is looked upon as the army of armies on foreign shores, is the opinion of Capt. Yoosuf, and everywhere that the boys land, no matter what the soil be, they are greeted effusively and treated royally.

Capt. Yoosuf has been in the service of the United States, 17 months. He was first stationed at Camp Devens and was later transferred to Fort Oglethorpe, Ga. He went to France with batteries 9, 10, 11, and 12, of the anti-aircraft forces. This is not the first time Capt. Yoosuf has been connected with war relief work. He went to Turkey in 1912 and 1913, and served at a Red Cross [Crescent] hospital in Constantinople during the Balkan War.

"I have passed a few days in the battle areas between the base ports of the British and the French fronts. I have traveled some hundreds of miles thru tracks of devastation. I have crossed Chateau Thierry, as far as Nancy, near Metz. On the way, I have seen long caravans of trucks of every description, mounted long guns, light artillery, tanks and everything else that traveled on wheels during the war.

113. Source: *Izgedda – Persian American Courier*, Vol. 4, No. 17, January 29 1919, p. 3. (*Editor*)

Captain Yoosuf in the service of the United States army. (Courtesy of George and Elsie Donabed Assyrian Collection and MARA.)

"Many of the places I have passed thru were scenes of absolute devastation and complete destruction. No devil could have completed a fiendish work as perfectly as the Huns did their ravaging of the French villages and cities. It is a terrible scene of village after village, especially around Amiens, Béthune, Péronne, Bapaume and Soissons. It is very hard for me to describe the appearance of these ruined villages.

"Some people in this country, and I might say the majority, believe that in the cases of these ruined villages, it is a village here and a village there, but sad to relate, such is not the case. There are chains of villages that have been destroyed, also some cities. The eastern and southern parts of France have not suffered as greatly as the opposite parts, but when one travels thru these sections of fair France, they are liable to see a house wrecked, or maybe a church steeple blown to atoms, or a part of a railroad station destroyed. The Huns have left detestable, souvenirs of their method of warfare in every section of France.

"There are spots of ruins which we were told were once prosperous cities, inhabited by happy and gay people who loved life and who had little thought of the great horror that was being planned some where in Germany. Now instead of being happy and peaceful communities, there is nothing but a mass of ruins, not a building standing, nor a tree left to raise its arms to heaven. The hardy hands of sinuous arms which built the masonry of great cathedrals, would behold nothing now but a few walls, standing, if they were to come back and behold the places where they lived.

"Any observer can realize that this destruction and devastation was not due to military reasons. It was due to mine explosions left by the retreating Huns. In my traveling, I saw hardly an orchard. Five years ago, there were forests and forests, but there are none now. Trees stand alone, now lifeless and leafless dead and burned. Vast fields full of gaps wide open, and many places full of graves. Even on the side of rail-road tracks, or near the fields, just a rude and simple wooden cross, to mark the spot, 'In Flanders fields, were poppies blow.'

"When we see those ruined villages, just piles of red dust, beyond repair, our minds become numb at the thought of rebuilding. This brings to the American people the stupendous work that lies before them. Americans, or even Frenchmen, cannot rebuild the centuries-old cathedrals, nor the historic chateaux nor houses. In the midst of these thoughts I was thinking 'Where have the people of these villages and cities gone?'

"I have seen refugees before, and I have seen them again going back to their homes. They are not slacking at the monstreous job that is before them. They are going back to their old homes to rebuild them.

"French people, the emotional, are rather stoic in some ways and are far from being despairing. They have been greatly hardened during the past four years, and what they have gone thru during this period. They have learned how to suffer, and they have learned how to endure. There is only one army, that is the American army. That is the army that is going to reconstruct these ruined cities and villages. The British and French and heroic Belgian armies are tired out. The American army is the only one left that is fit and capable of doing this great reconstruction work.

"The American army is greatly admired by the Allies. Many lips have uttered "The American army has saved us. American soldiers are so greatly admired that the minute they set foot on foreign soil, whether it be English or French or any other allied nation, the little boys and girls go marching with the troops from the ports to their resting camps, singing with the Yanks, "Over there," and carrying their shoulder guns or knapsacks.

"The American soldiers, those whom I have seen and I know those whom I have not seen, are glad to do their bit on the battlefield. They were anxious to go over the top and were courageous and fearless. There were times when they were even careless and just while they were careless, they might have accomplished some action which brought them the great praise from headquarters, or maybe a citation or decoration. I have seen them at the different hospitals where I have been stationed. No matter how bad their wounds were, they were at all times cheerful. When I would say to them simply, 'You are a hero' they would look at me and answer, just as simply, 'I had my duty to do.' They were satisfied to fight, knowing that they were fighting for a just cause, no matter what the final result would be.

"I was in a place near Liverpool called Knotty Ash, in camp hospital number 40. I remained there for three months and then received orders to rejoin batteries 9, 10, 11 and 12, which were due to go to the front. I was for a short time at a fort near Paris, called St. Steine. From there I went to a place called Le Bourget, which was a large airdrome. Here I saw thousands of airplanes of different types.

"While here I had the chance to fly, and so I did go up. I was in a plane which flew in the environs of Paris, over the city of Paris, over the Eiffel tower, and other places too numerous to mention. I went over the Seine also.

"I will say that the sensation one experiences in flying is peculiar, and, at first, I was a little scared, because I did not know the condition of flying.

"After leaving Le Bourget, we went to the Toul sector, a little north of the American army headquarters. Traveling is a little bit difficult. It would take us about four days to travel a distance of 400 kilometers. Accommodations were bad and even the officers were obliged to travel in a box car. We slept with straw under us and were packed in like sardines. Of course, we had no hot things to eat but were forced to live on cold beans and cold pressed meat. It really was a trying journey, but then we all had to do our bit for the great cause."

Captain Yoosuf is an Assyrian.

Assyrians Demand Independence with U. S. Protectorate[114]

Presbyterian Mission Board Accused by Speakers at Dinner of Promoting an Antagonistic Campaign

PROPOSALS FOR AN American protectorate over a new Assyria were cabled last night to President Wilson by representatives of the Assyrian population of the United States.

The aspirations of these people, whose territory includes parts of Mesopotamia and Persia, for an independent commonwealth, and their desire that the United States take it under its wing, were embodied in a resolution adopted at a dinner given by the Assyrian National Associations of America at the Hotel Pennsylvania. The banquet was in honor of Dr. Joel E. Werda, Assyrian delegate to the Peace Conference, who with Dr. A. K. Yoosuf, will place the aspirations of Assyrians in America before the peace table.

The 200 representatives, coming from all over the country, were somewhat startled by assertions of several speakers that the Presbyterian Board of Foreign Missions was bending every effort to thwart the national aims of the Assyrian people. The Persian Department of the board, they asserted, is conducting a systematic propaganda against them.

Persecution Is Charged

"We sincerely regret," said A. H. Oraham, a leading Assyrian, who was active securing the appointment of the delegates, "that while we have been redeemed from our first oppressors, we are now being subjected to the injustice of another autocracy, the Persian Department of the Presbyterian Board of Foreign Missions. It has persecuted our people,

114. Source: *New York Tribune*, Sunday, March 16, 1919, p. 4. (*Editor*)

165

pursued our leaders with hatred, conducted a secret propaganda against the fair name of our people, and has in every way opposed the work of our national organizations.

"It has tried to discredit the accomplishments of Assyrian leaders and has sent its agents into our colonies to arouse discord. It is impossible to enumerate all the deeds of injustice perpetrated against us by this board in America."

Mr. Oraham's remarks were supplemented by statements from Charles Dartley, secretary of the executive committee of the association, and Thomas Ellby, chairman of the Boston branch of the organization.

Declares Relief Work Opposed

Mr. Dartley spoke of the opposition experienced from the Presbyterian body. He said relief work among the Assyrians was opposed by the Presbyterian board, which suppressed their efforts and created a fund of its own, giving large sums to enemies of the Assyrians. He asserted the board also tried to prevent appointment of Assyrian delegates to the Peace Conference.

Dr. Werda, in outlining the program for the proposed new nation, believes it should comprise the 1,500,000 people now in that section and should not include the 750,000 Assyrians in India nor the 150,000 in Russia.

"It is the purpose of the Assyrian delegates in Paris," he said, "to claim a reasonable portion of the old Assyria which embraced, in its original boundaries, about 250,000 square miles. The Assyrians are entitled to this claim because Mesopotamia is their home, it is their land from generations back. They are entitled to it because they entered the war on the side of the Allies, and important victories were won by the Assyrian army.

"It is the purpose of the Assyrian delegates to ask for and insist upon the protectorate of the United States. The country presents marvelous and unique possibilities for American capital."

Letter from Mr. Shamsie of England[115]

DEAR MR. DARTLEY, Sec. Assyrian N. A'n

Thank you very much for your kind letter of the 30th inst. You say that you have just received two letters from your representatives in Paris. They inform you that the name of the new state is going to be Assyria-Chaldea, and that they had to concede to this point because five of the delegates from Turkey are Assyrian and Chaldean.

The above mentioned question came to my knowledge only on the 1st inst. I received two letters on that date, one from Mr. Werda and the other from Dr. Yoosuf. Both of them informed me about the matter, but Mr. Werda was decidedly opposed to the proposed name – Assyria-Chaldea.

On the 12th inst. I received a telegram from Dr. Yoosuf who had arrived in London, and he requested me to go up there expressly to meet him. I made the necessary arrangements with my employers and went up to see him. We had interviews with several men of high positions. The archbishop of Canterbury had made an appointment to see us; unfortunately, his letter was mislaid, and we could not keep the appointment, as he had to go away; but we saw his chaplain who took notes of all we said, and he presented them to the archbishop on his return. I am glad to say tht the chaplain said that his grace has done his utmost with our cause and that there has been accomplished more work in the Peace Conference with regard to Assyria, than we expected.

We also met Mr. Athelston Riley and put before him our claims. He promised to help our cause. We heard from another person who is in touch with the British officials, and he informed us that the general opinion with regard to Mesopotamia and the surrounding districts is that they should be known by their own name – Assyria.

I was in the company of Dr. Yoosuf some four days. We agreed that

115. Source: *The New Assyria*, Vol. III, No. 33, May 15, 1919, pp. 7–8. (*Editor*)

on his return to Paris, after our experience in London, he should hasten the delegates to present our claims at the Peace Conference and influence that the name of the new state should be Assyria, which is better than being Mesopotamia. As we finished our work, I returned on Saturday evening last, and Dr. Yoosuf had to leave for Paris on the following Sunday morning. I could not stay in London Saturday night on account of the scarcity of trains on Sunday.

I am very pleased to hear that you have had a number of interviews with the Archdeacon Creig, and that he promised to get the archbishop of Canterbury to aid our people.

One cannot say for certain how things will take place, but let us hope for the best way of securing the unity of our people.

Yours sincerely,

(Signed) SAID H. SHAMSIE

Capt. Yoosuf Pleads Assyrian Cause[116]

In a letter to Mr. George M. Hoyen, of 71 Charles Street, Capt. A. K. Yoosuf, M. D. writes of the necessity of rescuing Assyria completely from the baneful effects of Turkish rule. Dr. Yoosuf represents the Assyrians at the Peace Conference. In his letter he says:

The time is near when the democratic governments of the West will seriously consider the question of the Near East. The Supreme Council of the world Peace Conference is trying to solve the difficulty and complicated problems of the Near East – yes, trying to determine that this war be the last war. It will not be the last war unless they adjust the affairs rightly, and use the allied victory in such a way so as to remove certain causes of war.

Only a mere preaching of good will, the ideals of democracy, the wearing out of humanity from this present war and the economical conditions of the belligerent countries, will not be sufficient to prevent war in the future.

The Near East has been the scene of continual invasions, ebbing and flowing for centuries. The country has been saturated by continual bloodshed. The moral fortitude of the Christians alone has stood against the tides of extremities, and has heroically kept in existence through all the countries until this day.

The Assyrian hope does not see any Mongol or Tamerlane hordes sweeping across their country. They hope there will not be crusades or *jihads*. Neither will the massacres, pillaging and deportations be committed by the Turks.

At present every man with average intelligence in Europe and in America has some knowledge about Turkey. He is aware of the strategic importance of Constantinople. He knows also that the

116. Source: *The Lowell Sun Sunday Supplement*, September 7 1919, p. 5, second section. (*Editor*)

Christians in Turkey have been misgoverned for centuries. That Assyria is a fertile land, food producing land; he knows of the straits. He remembers the name of Gallipoli. The sacred city of Jerusalem. The Berlin-Bagdad railroad. The Bosphorus, The Sea of Marmora. In all, he knows the Turks, and their beautiful capital.

Why has Turkey lived so long? Some years ago his death sentence was uttered by European statesmen. Even by Gladstone, who called him the sick man of Europe. But nevertheless, he has lived long enough to demonstrate once more to the world and prove that he is still able to persecute and massacre the Christians – torture their wives, murder their innocent children and deport them to the deserts of Arabia.

There have been two reasons for his living. First, for the jealousy of the European powers which has been existent among them many years concerning Turkey and the straits. Second, the Turkish Government, realizing the above fact, has, for the last half century, been playing a clever diplomatic game with the European powers, to one giving the privileges of the railroads, and to another mortgaging the resources of the country.

Finance and intrigue have played a great role in the past. The European governments have been caring for this sick man for more than half a century. The Turk has been holding Constantinople because no one nation dare to trust another with so great a prize. Whether the Peace Conference decides that the sultan will reside at Constantinople or not it is a matter of consequence. The Allied democracy ... be responsible for the fair way. They must have a strong power or sea which will put its authority beyond all doubt.

This war has proven exclusively that Turkey's power must ... to an end in Asia. The question then naturally will arise, what will become of the Christians in Turkey? To redeem them from the ... of the Turks, and give them autonomy under the European power for a period. Second, do not let Turkey dominate Constantinople, Dardanelles and the Bosphorus. The present ... of the Allies intention toward the solution of the Turkish empire is right. ... This is the only solution. This political cancer must be cut off. This is the only cure.

Constantinople and the Dardanelles should be made international. If the Allies expect peace in the Near East, the old financial and economic system must be abolished. Concessions, loans, exploitations, etc., should be decided in the open by a body of persons who command the respect of the world.

Reforms under the Turkish rule must be dismissed as hopeless. The history for the last hundred years has been a history of reform written in the blood of Assyrians. Their massacres, deportations, and imprisonments are the proofs of extermination of the Assyrians. But the hand of Providence has been working against such an abominable policy.

The beautiful land of Assyria which is, and will be, a food producing country with an ... future for agriculture has been laid waste. Under any rule and with any population but that of the Turk, it would be a paradise.

The Turks may claim and maintain a Turkish state and promise real guarantees for the lives and the properties of the Assyrians, but such a claim cannot be accepted. The past century's promises and reforms have been a failure. The Assyrians have been crushed under the heels of injustice and barbarism committed by the Kurds. The Kurdish chiefs have been encouraged and decorated for their wrong deeds by the Turkish Government. The very same Kurds, the enemies of the Assyrians who have destroyed their sanctuaries, demolished their properties and live upon the labor of the Assyrian populace, the Kurds who have fought against democracy of the Allied powers, are demanding freedom.

To permit Turkey to occupy his original state, to create a new Kurdish state, and to establish an Arab kingdom will be one of the greatest misfortunes for the Assyrians residing among them.

The Assyrians in Turkey and Persia have fought the Allied battle, sacrificing everything, saturating the earth with their blood for the sake of emancipation and liberty, and for the sake of the land in which they live. The national revival of the nomad Kurd and the retarded Arab of the desert will not be able to throw away their old nature. It will take years to educate and cultivate them, while the Assyrians are ready to follow the path of democracy. They are ready to adopt western civilization. The Kurd have stood as a barrier against civilization, against humanity. Those who have fought against Christian institutions, today they are demanding recognition before the great tribunal of the world.

A. K. YOOSUF, M. D.

The Fitchburg Convention[117]

WE DO NOT know when and where we have felt so proud of an Assyrian Colony as we did of this body of the Assyrian men and women who reside in the city of Fitchburg, Mass. It was to the credit of our brethren from Turkey to have had such a representation of the prominent American element present in the convention. We felt equally proud in seeing our esteemed Brother Dr. A. K. Yoosuf in the uniform of a lieutenant of the U.S. Army.

Dr. Yoosuf, as the chairman, opened the convention by an eloquent address, speaking of the qualities of the Assyrian people and their desirability as American citizens.

After the chairman's remarks, the Honorable Frank Foss, the mayor, honored the convention by appropriate remarks which kindled fresh patriotic enthusiasm in the hearts of the hearers. It indeed proves the high esteem in which the Assyrians of Fitchburg have been by the population of the city where they have made their homes. For, in addition to the presence of the mayor, the Honorable Judge Gallagher also delivered a short but stirring address. Rev. A. J. Gammack swayed the audience by another eloquent address when he spoke of the duty of the Assyrians in the present conflict into which America has entered for the liberation of small nations.

Mr. E. A. Onthank, the leading banker of Fitchburg, sent his telegraphic regrets for his unavoidable absence, and also his hearty congratulations for the convention.

We had attended similar gatherings before, and we had previously witnessed some great patriotic demonstrations; but it surely is to the credit of worthy leaders of this colony when words were put into deeds by voluntary sacrifices made upon the national altar and for the national treasury. The piles of money given in contributions of love

117. Source: *The New Assyria*, Vol. II, No. 14, October 15 1917, pp. 4–5. (*Editor*)

and patriotism were simply amazing. A colony that has such leaders as George Bros., and Mr. Harry Peters and other cannot help but be a credit to the fair name of the Assyrian Nation.

Here was laid another cornerstone of independence of the Assyrian nation! *

The contributions at the Fitchburg convention amounted to $150.

Presidents Answer to the Resolutions of the Assyrian Convention in Fitchburg, Mass.

The White House

Washington

Oct. 13, 1917

My dear Sir:-

The President asks me to acknowledge receipt, and to express his warm appreciation of your telegram of the 12th inst. of a convention of Assyrians of New England.

With warm thanks to you and to all thoses concerned, I am

Sincerely yours,

H. TUMULTY

Sec. to the President

First Lt. A. K. Yoosuf

Base Hospital

Camp Devens, Mass.

Asks Aid For People
– Dr. Yoosuf Says Assyrians Were
Promised Mesopotamia by Allies[118]

ASSISTANCE FOR THE Assyrian-Chaldean people, inhabitants of the Tigris-Euphrates Valley, who have been persecuted by Persians and Turks, has been asked by Dr. A. K. Yoosuf, of Worcester, Mass., major in the United States Army and now president of the Assyrian-Chaldean National Unity organization.

"My countrymen have been martyred by the Turks in Asia Minor and Mesopotamia ever since the war, when they fought on the side of the Allies," Dr. Yoosuf said. "My people claim Mesopotamia, but since the end of the war, it has been divided between the French and English. Our country was promised an allotment of land, but it has never gotten it. The Allies should live up to their promise."

He said the Assyrians were scattered all over Armenia, Turkey, Persia and Russia. They have no complete freedom and are forced by circumstances to be practically a nomad race.

The Assyrians and Chaldeans in this country have organized and will shortly conduct a drive for funds. The headquarters are in Newark, N J.

118. Source: *Philadelphia Enquirer*, Thursday Morning, March 24, 1921, p. 12. (*Editor*)

174

The Man About Town[119]

WE HAVE HEARD much about the sufferings of Armenia and her people, both as a result of the World War and for many years before. A Lowell man who knows much about the Assyrians through many years of association with them calls my attention to an able article in a recent issue of the New Assyria, a magazine published in Jersey City, NJ, signed by Dr. A.K. Yoosuf, who is a delegate to the Peace Conference from the Assyrian National Association of this country in which the need of justice and aid for Assyria just as much as for Armenia is emphasized. Lowell Assyrians will be interested in Dr. Yoosuf's work at the Conference and the closing paragraph of his article sums up his entire appeal to the people of the United States: "Give them a chance, and they will prove to the world their ability as fighters, as administrators, as educators. They are the sons and daughters of the mighty kingdom of Assyria."

<hr>

119. Source: *The Lowell Sun*, Saturday May 17, 1919, p. 6. (*Editor*)

Third Annual Pic-Nic[120]

THE UNIQUE PIC-NIC of the Assyro-Chaldean National Unity of Boston branch for the benefit of the *Union* took place on Sunday Sept. 4th, 1921.

The gathering of more than 300 Assyrians from all colonies; the sunny day made the Pic-Nic a real and unique one.

The Pic-Nic opened by the president of the said unity Mr. Thos. Ellbey, who thanked the people and expressed his wishes for good enjoyment.

The second speaker, the president of the headquarters of the said organizations Major A. K. Yoosuf, spoke in regards of Assyro-Chaldean, and assured the people, by pointing that the freedom of Assyro-Chaldean depend on the people of our nation more than on the representatives of the nation.

And while the representatives are working, the nation should back them up, by doing so, if not to-day sure, positively some day in the near future will enjoy the freedom in our own country.

Regards to the *Union* publication, our well known eloquent speaker Major A. K. Yoosuf, expressed his words in such a way that if ever there happened to be an Assyrian who has not become a subscriber of the publication, would become one at that same time.

Our efforts are like flames of the kerosene he said, if we keep it burning, we will see the flames, if not, the whole flames will die and even once there has been a fire. Now if we work hard to keep this publication running, we will have a newspaper in Assyrian for long years, if not, some day we may lose this lovely gift and left without it. Same we were for centuries.

Mr. Francis Em. Hoyen, presented a group picture of Assyro-

120. Source: *The Union – Official Organ of Assyro-Chaldean National Unity of America*, Vol. I, No. 12, September 10, 1921, p. 4. (*Editor*)

The Union – Official Organ of Assyro-Chaldean National Unity of America. Right: Francis Emmanuel Hoyen.(Courtesy of MARA.)

Chaldean National Unity branch of Fresno, Cal. in a gathering of National Pic-Nic, and upon his wishes the same was auctioned by Mr. Thos. Ellbey and Major A. K. Yoosuf, which brought over forty dollars, and won by Mr. John Thalbash. The collection of said photo went to the A. C. N. U.

The most events of the enjoyment were the Assyrian and Hellenic dances, which hypnotized the people, while were danced by Assyrian and Hellenic well dancers.

The people were so satisfied with the management of the Pic-Nic that they many times expressed their wishes for holding such Pic-Nics in the future summers.

At 8 PM the Pic-Nic was closed by the president, by thanking the people for their encouragement, and also thanking the workers and management of the Pic-Nic who sacrificed their good time and comfort in order to entertain the gathering.

N. B. Quoyoon.

Word[121] has come to Dr. A. K. Yoosuf, the president of the Assyrian-Chaldean Union, that some sixty two Assyrians were imprisoned in Samsun on the Black Sea by Kemal Pasha's regime, and that they are released and are now in Constantinople stranded and unable to secure a passport. They had left their home in Harpoot long before they had ever heard of the new immigration law.

121. Source: *The Union – Official Organ of Assyro-Chaldean National Unity of America*, Vol. I, No. 20, November 5, 1921, p. 4. (*Editor*)

Prospects in California[122]

A CORRESPONDENT WRITES from San Francisco that "California is the real place for our people. It is a land of milk and honey;" every word of it is true. For you can find no other climate in all the world like California's, and fine fruits excel any thing which I have seen....

But of course our people must understand that they have to work. California or any other American farm cannot be made a success by lazy people, even if you give it free to them. If the government will take particular interest in our people and allow them land on terms of fifteen to twenty five years and locate them in some fairly good tract of lands and encourage them to become selfsupporting and good citizens, there is no reason at all why our people will not succeed. Such men must, in addition, be men of character, courage and never be afraid of work. Such people as Gulpashan, Geogtapa and others who have some experience in raising vineyards and orchards ought to make a good material to start.

Dr. A. K. Yoosuf, the president of the Assyro-Chaldean National Union went to Washington recently to consult on the prospects of getting into America some sixty or more Assyrians now in Constantinople who were detained by Mustapha Kemal Pasha during the activities of the Nationalists. Dr. Yoosuf says that he saw the authorities who showed him every kind of consideration and also appeared before the immigration committees[123] whom Mr. Knightly has been interviewing with a great deal of success.

---

122. Source: *The Union – Official Organ of Assyro-Chaldean National Unity of America*, Vol. I, No. 28, December 31, 1921, p. 4. (*Editor*)

123. The statement of Dr. A. K. Yoosuf before the immigration committees is included in this book, see previous chapter. (*Editor*)

The Corner Stone Welfare Council – Its Services to Humanity[124]

THE ACHIEVEMENTS OF the CORNER STONE WELFARE COUNCIL INC. of Boston, Washington and New York for the welfare of the Assyrian immigrants during the past few months have been extraordinary. The Assyrian-Chaldean Union, therefore, on its fifth annual convention at Boston invited Mr. Daniel A. Mackay the president of the Council, and Mr. C. V. Knightly to a dinner given at the Adams House on Saturday evening November 26th; to our regret, Mr. MacKay, who is an orator of wonderful talent and great powers, is hardly left alone, and he had to fill another engagement the same day elsewhere. The Union was therefore delighted with the presence of the Welfare counselor who graced the head of the table together with Dr. A. K. Yoosuf, the President, who as our readers well know served in France in the American army.

Dr. Yoosuf spoke of the great services and sacrifices of the Assyrians in the war, and the defense they had made for the Allies' cause, but that today they found themselves with the Armenians without any home and almost without any hopes. But he was glad to know and to learn of the services of the Corner Stone Welfare Council through its devoted spokesman who was our honored guest.

124. Source: *The Union – Official Organ of Assyro-Chaldean National Unity of America*, Vol. I, No. 30, January 14, 1922, p. 4. (*Editor*)

Physician Drops Dead in His Office –
Dr. A.K. Yoosuf Prominent in Worcester[125]

Special Dispatch to the Globe

WORCESTER, Dec. 27 – Dr Arthur K. Yoosuf, 56, one of the most prominent physicians in this city, dropped dead last night in his office at 93 Austin St. Death was caused by heart disease. Dr Yoosuf had been a practicing physician in this city for many years and was widely known among Assyrian residents throughout New England.

During the World War, he served as a major in the medical corp and was commended by the Government for his service. He also served as a medical officer during the Balkan Wars. Dr. Yoosuf was an energetic worker for the interest of Near East immigrants who arrived in this section of the country.

During the drive for funds for Near East Relief, he gave of his time and money to the project practically ceasing his practice to assist.

The Assyrian and Armenian colonies in this city were thrown into despair when the death of Dr. Yoosuf became known. He had just been out on a call and came back to his office, complaining that he was ill. His sister, Mary, said that he seated himself in a chair and then dropped to the floor and when she reached his side he was dead.

Besides being a member of many Assyrian organizations, he was an officer in the medical division of the Veterans of Foreign Wars.

125. Source: *Boston Daily Globe*, December 27, 1924. (*Editor*)

Noted Surgeon is Stricken[126]

Worcester, Mass., Dec. 27 – Dr. Arthur K. Yoosuf, who won fame as a surgeon in both the Balkan and World Wars, died suddenly in his office here last night. His death was caused by heart disease. Overwork in connection with the erection of a new Assyrian church, coupled with a large practice, is thought to have caused his death.

Dr. Yoosuf was born in Harpoot, Asiatic Turkey, in 1867, and came to New York in 1889.

In the Balkan War, he was chief operating surgeon in a hospital in Constantinople and was later decorated by the sultan of Turkey for meritorious service. In the World War, Dr. Yoosuf served as a major in the United States Medical Corps.

---

126. Source: *Syracuse Herald*, 1924. (*Editor*)

PART VI

FACSIMILE OF
THE PARIS REPORT

TO THE EXECUTIVE COMMITTEE OF A.N.A.

Gentlemen,

Permit me to bring to the attention of Ex. Committee a
brief report of my work as a representative of Assyrians in
America to the Peace Conference at Paris and France.

After arriving at America from the American Expeditionary
Force in France, I was approached by a few gentlemen asking me
to go to France to represent the Assyrian Cause. Without
hesitation I have accepted the offer thinking that it is my
duty to serve for my poor nation, in such a time when there is a
struggle for freedom for every nation. I was under the impression
that everything was ready for presenting our cause to the Peace
Conference - our losses and the number of massacred people - that
the Committee was in touch with the people in Turkey or in Persia
concerning the claims of our nation.

After having had experience with the British Consulate
as regards visaing our passports for London, we secured the visa
of the French Consulate and left the city of New York before
your President, for Paris on March 8th 1919 (Saturday) on the
S. S. "Raterdam" arriving at Havre on March 18th at 11.30 a.m.
We left Havre for Paris at 6.30 p.m. and arrived at Paris 1.30
a.m. on March 19th 1919.

For the first few days I tried to locate the delegates of
the Peace Conference of the Allied Nations. I visited His
Excellency Noubar Pacha where I met Mr. Melcolm, who gave me some
important information. I also met Armenian Delegates from
different parts of Turkey. Prof. Hachadoorian who had just
arrived from Bakuba informed me that two delegates - General
Agha Pitros and Lady Sourma Marshimoon-will represent the people
of Bakuba in Paris at the Peace Conference.

From now on, my work was to locate the delegates of Allied
Nations and see them if possible. It was not an easy task in
those days to see them, while everyone was busy. During my
interview with Noubar Pacha, His Exellency made the remark of
trying to make Armenians and Assyrians a Federal Government, but,
of course, I could not answer this question without consulting with
others. However, Mr. Melcolm interceding said that the clergy in
England were trying to make an Assyrian Province, which ended the
matter. However, all the Armenian Delegates have expressed their
sympathy and wished their sister nation, Assyria, was also
free from the Turkish yoke.

March 24th 1919. Visited Sir Robert Cecil at the Hotel Astoria -
the office of the British Delegate. After explaining my mission to
him he told me to see r. Toyneee who had charge of the Asiatic
questions in Turkey.

March 25th 1919. Visited Mr. J. C. Grews, Secretary of the Peace

Conference for American Delegation. He took me to Mr. Leon
Domminion who is the head of the Eastern division. After
explaining to him my mission, he told me that the American
Government would not allow his citizens to represent their
native country as a delegate. I immediately wrote a letter
to the Secretary, Mr. Crew, on this matter, which he answered
saying that I might work as a _representative_ for Assyrian
Cause.

March 27th 1919. I had an interview with Mr. Toynbee, the head
of the British Delegate. I told him the Assyrians' demand and
showed to him the boundaries of the territories we are demanding.
He agreed with me in all the claims, also asking a state or
a province independent Assyria, but he suggested not to define
the the boundaries as it would be at the hand of the Peace Conference
deciding this matter. While I was interviewing the American
experts on Asia Turkey Prof. McGae, Prof. Wiseman and Mr. Montgomery
asked me for a preparatory or a preliminary memorandum, sothat
they would know the Assyrians' claims. I complied with their demand
and prepared a short memorandum stating our claims and boundaries
under the three headings:-

    (1)   Freedom from Turkish and Persian Yoke.
    (2)   Reparation of Indemnities.
    (3)   Establishment of an Independent Assyrian State under
          one Mandate.

    I delivered these preliminary memoranda to the Allied
Delegates. I entered in this brief memorandum the Assyrian
boundaries according to the wish of American experts.

April 1st 1919. I was informed the arrival of the Delegates of
Assyria-Chaldeans at the Hotel Powers. I hurriedly went there to
see them. Really they are find looking men, influential and
intelligent.

April 4th 1919. With our Asseyro-Chaldean Delegates visiting
American Delegates. I told them my preliminary work.

April 6th 1919. (Sunday) The Assyro-Chaldean Colleagues called
upon the President of A.N.A. at one hotel, where we had some
informal talks during which it was asked how much the Assyrians in
America could give for the cause of propaganda and also talked
about the name - no decision.

April 8th 1919. Had an informal meeting - no President and no
Secretary. We agreed upon the name of _Assyro-Chaldean_. At this
meeting our Colleagues told us that their interest was for the
nation alone and for her freedom - no religious influence had
to do with them, it was purely national. That was all we talked
again of propaganda, and that Assyrians in America alone cannot
dictate in this matter. A little later on Mr. Erde refused to
be called Asseyro-Chaldean. I have tried to convince him of the
necessity of adopting this name, which for the sake of union,
which will not hurt our cause. Secondly I have tried to show him

that Assyrians in America along cannot dictate in this matter and
I do not believe any Catholic influence will enter into this matter.
If the British get the mandate, what will the Catholic influence
amount to ? But our Colleagues assured us that their mission is
not religious, but for the nation's freedom and liberty.

April 14th 1919.   Made an arrangement to see Col. House.

April 21st 1919.   Saw Mr. Melcolm with Mr. Werda and after a long
conversation he gave us a letter of introduction to Col. Gribbon,
who has considerable knowledge about Mesopotamia and Urmia. We
asked his advice how to put a claim in our memorandum against
Persia and also about boundaries. He, evading the question, told
us to write a letter to His Exellency A.T.Willson, Chief Political
Office of India.

April 23rd 1919.   Mr. Werda and myself visited His Excellency Persian
ex Minister of Foreign Affairs. There was considerable talk about
the Persian attitude during the war.

April 25th 1919.   With Mr. Namik visited Mr. Grey and asked him
to give some information with regard to preparing a map in connection
with our claims.

April 28th 1919.   An informal meeting at theHotel Powers at 4 p.m.
Mr. Werda was not present. I tried to make the Meeting regular by
appointing a President and a Secretary, but the full members not
being present it was left aside.

April 30th 1919.   I accompanied Mr. Werda and visited Mr. Grey,
American expert in regard to Persia, to get to know something about
Persian and Turkish boundaries and to ask his advice as to how to
prepare the claim.

    Mr. Werda is suspicious of the name of Assyro-Chaldean and not
anxious to meet them. He thought of writing a letter to the
Archbishop of Canterbury regarding Assyro-Chaldean name and asking
his influence in this respect when the Assyrians'fate is decided.

    This caused the first beark of working together. No union,
and no harmony.

May 5th 1919.   We had a long talk with Mr. Forbes Adams in regard
to Mesopotamia. He said he could not say very much then, but very
likely the Peace Conference would make an AUTONOMOUS MESOPOTAMIA
giving privileges to Christians there. "This is only a British idea"
he said.

    After talking of my visit to London with Mr. Werda and our
Chaldean brothers, it was decided that I should go to London.

May 11th 1919. Left Paris for London. On my way to Boulogne
I had the pleasure and the honour of meeting Mr. Lancing, Secretary
of the State, with whom I had a delightful conversation. I told
him about the Assyrians - their past and present state; their fight
on the side of the Allies and their sufferings. He said "If the
times comes I shall remember the Assyrian Cause and will do all

...can for your cause people, but, he added, there is Kurdish
question" I tried to enlighten his mind on this matter
explaining the Kurds and their character etc.

May 13th 1919. (In London) I immediately began to visit some
prominent persons who had connection with the Mesopotamia Affairs.
I had talks with Sir James Smith, Major Young and with the Hon.
Arthur Hertzel at the Indian Office, who listened carefully. He
said something about the Kurdish question and also informed me that
Marshemwon had already forwarded the claims of his people asking
British protection. Surely, he said, the Assyrian question will
come before the Peace Conference and they will decide the best thing
for the Assyrians. I brought to his attention Urmea's sufferings
and her claims for indemnity. In answer, he said "Persia is a neutral
country and we can niether consider it at the Peace Conference nor
fix the Indemnities, but, he said, the Allied Government and
particularly the British Government has made some arrangement with the
Persian Government for the payment of Indemnities.

With Mr. Said Shemsie I visited Assyrian friend Mr. Athalston
Riley and thanked him for his sympathy toward Asseyrians. Of course
he said he would do all he could to help the Assyrian cause. I asked
him to organise a committee for Assyro-Chaldeans, to which he
promised to do his best.

I visited the Archbishop of Canterbury. In his absence I
had a talk with his private secretary who wrote down all my sayings.
I told him that it was a national question and not a secterian affair.
ALL ASSYRIA DEMANDING FREEDOM.

I called upon Rev. Heaxill at Crayton with Mr. Shemsie.
He has been to Urmia - Joulemarg Hikiary. He knew the Assrians well
and spoke about them very sincerely. I told him the wish of all the
Assyrians, which was for freedom and the establishment of an
independent state under one Power. He has some influence at the
Foreign Office.

What I gathered from the conversations I had with these
gentlemen was the recognition of the Kurdish element.

Paris

May 28th 1920. (Paris) I suggested that we divide the Mesopotamia
into difference districts, showing in each district our majority,
e.g. Diarhiker, Mussal, Urmia and Euphrates.

June 4th 1920. Wrote a letter to the Archbishop of Canterbury
reminding him of our just and right Cause and of His Grace's
influence of speech in the House of Lords in regard to the Assyrians.

June 12th 1920. There is more talk about the Kurdish question.

Hamdy Bey and Sherif Pacha are here for the Kurdish Cause.

was
      The name Assyro-Chaldean/again brought up. It seems to me
that our Jacobite brothers accepted this name at the beginning
at Constantinople. "It is a pitiful thing indeed" said one of the
Delegates "that you think this is a religious movement" I said
emphatically "No".

June 11th 1919. I met the Delegates from Caucasia and Urmia -
Priest Lazor George, Lazor Yaṙhoff, Shimon Geuge and Dr. ~~Jusia W~~ *Jessie*
Yonan.

June 16th 1919. I arranged a Meeting for all the Delegates to be
present at Hotel Powers. Mr. Werda was not present. At this
Meeting Prof. Yahannan spoke about Urmia. I told the Meeting
of our doings in regard to Assyria's freedom and also said that
we were preparing a Memorandum which I hoped would be satisfactory
to all the Delegates.

      To make the Meetings regular, I proposed to form a real organisa-
tion, with a President, Secretary and Treasurer, but no one seconded
my motion and everybody said "What is the difference ? We are all
working toward one end. But it is not the way to represent a nation
without an organisation or without a bureau. On such an occasion every
one will call upon the Members of the Peace Conference telling them
they are Delegates and presenting something different than the others.
This is surely a folly and worse, it is an insane idea and not a
business way. I made a motion that Assyro-Chaldean Delegates have
a place, which shall be recognised by the Peace Conference and by the
Allied Governments. I did not succeed in doing so as we could not
decide who was the legitimate Delegate. A case happed in recognising
Prof. Yohannan. How could we refuse to let him attend the Mee ting
when all the others had not shown their credentials, and to whom
will they show their credentials and who are representing ?

June 18th 1919. We tried to have a meeting again this morning
(9.45 a.m.) There were not many present.

June 20-21. 1919. Two informal Meetings at the Hotel Powers when
Dr. Jesie Yonan read some part of his prepared documents relating
to the Assyrians' acceptance of the written promises of the Allied
Representatives to join the armies of the Allied Governments. *&c.*

June 23rd 1919. All the Delegates were present at the Hotel Powers.
Dr. Yonan again spoke against the attitude of the British Government.
He said he had proofs that the British had forced Marshimoon and Malek
Hooshaba to abide with the English decision - there was a unanimous
belief that Marshimoon and Malek Hooshaba cannot decide the destiny
of their people. I had proposed for an immediate action, but to be
able to present such an urgent matter it ought to go through our
official body. *which we did not have it*

June 25th 1919. Prof. Yohannan at today's Meeting at the Hotel Powers
(8 p.m.) prepared a petition to present to the Peace Conference in
regard to the Assyrians in Persia, but Mr. Namrk and myself objected
to this. *The petition was on the line of returning of the Assyrians of Bakubah, we*
We argued that his it not the time for their return to their Roads, for the reason
of the present dangerous situation, and the attitude of the Kurds.

<u>June 29th 1919.</u> A Meeting at the Hotel Powers (9 p.m.) at which
Mr. Werda was not present. Dr. Yonan prepared an appeal
for an immediate help to those suffering Assyrians in Persia
and Caucasia. I was authorised to see the President of the Relief
Committee in the Near East and the American Red Cross and other
places if necessary, presenting to them the real need of those
Assyrians in those parts who were destitute and without help.

For the Relief Work, I called upon Major Carbin and Col. R. E.
Alots of the Red Cross. From there I went to see Col. Payson and
he told me that the American Red Cross had turned the work in
that section over to the Near East Relief Committee. I then saw
Mr. Hoover and Mr. Morganstow and they both told me that, though
things were in a very bad form, they believed that within a short
time everything would be in a better condition, and that the
Relief Committee would be able to look after the Assyrians.

Mr. Morganthow promised to consult Mr. Hoover today regarding
my request and arrange matters.

<u>July 2nd 1919.</u> I had an interview with Mr. Forbes Adams, one
of the British Delegates, who expressed the sympathy towards the
Assyrians and emphasised the fact that the British Government
realised its responsibility and that, if America took the
mandate of Armenia they would gladly take the mandate of the
whole of Mesopotamia.

<u>July 3rd 1919.</u> Received a cable from America asking me why Mar
Shimoon and others could not come to Paris. Have Send Telegrams:

<u>July 11th 1919.</u> Expecting Delegates. There was some trouble
over the signing of our claims. On account of the disagreement
concerning the name, we were, naturally, working separately and
in consequence I could not receive the statistics, and the map
from our Colleagues as they were using them themselves.
Our Chaldean Delegates, thinking that Turkish question will
not come within at least a few months time, have left for
Constantinople and will return to Paris later on.

<u>July 21st 1919.</u> (Monday) Our published claims are ready this
morning and I received a letter from Mr. George in the Assyrian
language, but its publication was delayed as it required approving
and signing by all the seven delegates including Prof. Yohannan.
There was some difficulty, but I undertook the charge if they
could agree. Dr. Jassé Yonan and Mr. George objected about the
numbers and the exaggerated statements as "laying down the foundations
of Universities and schools and National Treasury etc. To this
last question I answered that it was not a question of how much
money the Treasury has at present. I tried to bring these gentlemen
to some understanding with Mr. Werda, but the terrible personal
dislikes were playing such a great roll that it was injuring the
National Cause. The Presbyterian questions were again brought out.
Really this and other unimportant questions were seen brought out.
National crises like this.

I offered to accept their suggestions in regard to some
points and I asked them for consideration in regard to their
supplimentary note which they were to present to the Peace
Conference:-

    (1) That they would not send it.
    (2) If they did send it, it must be in accordance with
        our demand for claims.

In this respect Prof. iohanan agreed to write a letter for the
recognition of A.N.A. and we agreed to sign their supplementary
memorandum of they would sign ours. I even took the responsibility
(rather "precaution") of making rubber stamps for their names.

After reading the memorandum of Dr. Jusie Yonan and Prof.
Yohanan, Mr. Werda refused to sign it. I could not see any harm
in signing the Memorandum of both gentlemen as it dealt merely
with an appeal for the need of Persian Assyrians. The same
nature of Memorandum was also given to the Peace Conference by
Mr. Lazar Yacaboff for the immediate relief of Cacasian
Assyrians.

July 21st 1919. (4 p.m.) At Dr. Jessie's room - not all present.
Neither Mr. Werda. I tried to arrange another meeting for July 22nd.
On this date again at Dr. Yonan's room at Rue Londers. Present -
Prof. Yohanan, Dr. Yonan, Mr. Genje and myself. In this meeting
I proposed to create a union between Urmia gentlemen to work in
unison for the sake of national prosperity and freedom. I proposed
also to arrange a Committee for the relief work for the suffering
people in different regions and, if possible, to choose some one
familiar with the conditions in Urmia, Salmas, our fight etc.
to lecture in England and in America. They all agreed upon this
but no action took place on account of both parties refusing to
sign alternately the memoranda without change.

July 27th 1919. Sunday Meeting in London Palace Hotel.
Present - Dr. Jessie Yonan, Prof. Yohanan, Mr. Genje and Priest
Lazar George. Prof. Yohanan read special news from the American
State Department on the latest massacres of Urmia. We thought to
bring such important incidents to the attention of the public, but
for this we must have a publicity bureau. The Urmian Delegates
brought out the question of the Protectorate of Persian Assyrian.
After considering the pros and cons I suggested that, Urmia being
a neutral country, we could not ask from the Peace Conference
direct protection, but we might ask for a way to be provided
which would influence the Persian Government to look after the
Assyrians, or ask the British Government to use her influence for
those Assyrians until these pending questions were finally settled.
by the Peace Conference.
    Priest George received a cable from Chicago asking him if Dr.
Yonan and Prof. Yohannan had been sent out from the meeting of
Assyrian Delegates and whether Priest Lazar George had joined Mr.
Werda. We suggested that he answer this cable in the negative
and say that they were Delegates.

It seems to me that there are very foolish things in circulation among the Assyrians in America.'

Our Urmian Delegates were anxious that the emmigrants in Bakuba and in Russia were sent to their respective places and homes. In reference to this matter I approached the British Members of the Peace Conference for advice. He told me that it was not the time to send them to their homes as things were not settled and there was more danger. The very same thing was discussed at one of our Meetings and Mr. Namik's suggestion to leave the matter to the judgment of the British Government was unanimously accepted.

<u>July 28th 1919.</u> I delivered our claims personally to all the Allied Delegates and to the Secretary of the Peace Conference; and sent others to the London Foreign and Indian Offices, Archbishop of Canterbury and many other places including America.

All eyes in American are looking here for a light. Every heart is throbbing for news of Assyrian-Chaldean freedom. I would like to send a message of good news but I am not in a position to tell anything definite. I will keep up my conversative views and not dope my people with imagination. I have seen Mr. White, the president of American Delegates and also Sir Craw, the secretary of the British Delegates. Both spoke with hope of Christian deliverance.

<u>August 1st 1919.</u> (Saturday) While I was on my way to see the American Delagte and the expert on Persia, I met Prof. Yohannan who was waiting for Dr. Yonan. We all went together to see Mr. Gray. Of course, the whole topic was Persian Assyrians and their sufferings.

Dr. Yonan asked Mr. Grey why the Allies could not send a few thousand soldiers to protect them. Mr. Grey answering, said that no Government would send soldiers there, adding that all Assyrians did not go to Mesopotamia. I had an interview with Gen. ratin who referred us to Mr. Balfour. It is evident that the southern part of Mesopotamia will be under British Control.

I received a letter from Assyrian fives advising me to go to Constantinople to end the difficulties. I answered that I would not be able to go without the permission of the Ex. Committee.

<u>August 5th 1919.</u> I visited Mr. Van Sittery, British Delagate expert on the Turkish question and told him of our claims and sufferings. He spoke very nicely about Assyro-Chaldeans question assuring me that the Peace Conference would take the Assyro-Chaldean question into consideration. During this time there was some massacre going around just yet I told him that it was the duty of the English Government to protect them as she had the power and the influence. If she has not sufficient soldiers then why not arm the natives, train them and give them ammunition and arms to protect themselves, as such things as massacres will happen until the country is settled. He said it was a good idea and asked me to put it into writing. he said it would be a good idea to talk about this matter with Mr. Buclim

the American expert. Mr. Buclin did not approve the idea at first
thinking that:-

(1) It would be difficult to transport ammunition *and guns*

(2) It would arouse the hatred of the surrounding Kurdish
     tribes and they would massacre the remain̶d̶e̶r̶ *ning Assyrians*.

Seeing that the Turkish question would not come within a short
time and realising also the financial situation in America, I thought
with true feeling that <u>one man was enough here</u>, and I suggested this
to the Executive Committee.

I had heard many unpleasant things reported from Paris to the
Committee. It is too bad that things have not been reported to the
people in their true light. After all my endeavours I am deeply sorry
that I was not able to bring the Urmian people together, as there
was always some unpleasant remarks about each other. Surely, I
thought, our Nestorian brothers know each other very well, so I left
the matter to take its course.

<u>August 12th 1920.</u> I had another interview with Mr. Van Sittart.
I asked him if Assyrian question would come before the Peace Conference.
He answered "Yes", but not as the Armenian question, as Assyrian
question will be settled between the two governments, most probably
Asseyro-Chaldean having some kind of autonomy " Surely both the
Governments acknowledge the services your people have rendered
during the war. In regard to Dearbekir and Mardin, I expressed
my feeling strongly and also proved that in that region the majority
are Assyro-Chaldeans. We are not asking either for charity or a
favor, but our right.

Corresponding with the Archbishop of Canterbury and with Rev.
Heasel of Croyden. *England*

<u>September 11th - 15th.</u> There is some contradictory statements and
disputes going on between Priest Lazar George, Mr. Genje and Mr. Werda;
the conversations being in Assyrian I was not able to understand.
Some letters also passed between Mr. Werda and Priest Lazar
George and Mr. Genja.

<u>September 15th 1919.</u> Visited the British Prime Minister where I
found Mr. Churchill and Col. Gribbon. I had a long talk with the
Secretary of the Prime Minister, Mr. Philip Karr. After a great deal
of talk about our situation, our claims, boundaries etc? I asked what
I should write to my people. "Write just what our conversation has been"
I have already written this conversation to the Ex. Committee under the
date of Sept. 15th 1919.

I paid Priest Lazor and Mr. Ganja some amount for their journey
and also Lazar Yacohoff.

During this period I was corresponding with the National Council
at Constantinople. The trouble between Patriarch and Council is known
to the Committee.

October 12th 1919. Mr. Namik is back from Constantinople and I had a talk with him in regard to the affairs at Constantinople.

There is news of Patriarch's coming to Paris, but no news from Constantinople.

October 27th 1919. I expect the arrival of Siverious Mutran Afram Barso-Paris - On every occasion I had interviews with different persons I found out that they all said complimentary things for Assyro Chaldeans and promised to do whatever they could. There was talk that the French will occupy Cilesia and upper Mesopotamia as far as Harbout. I am told by an American delegation, Mr. Crey that at present there is a universal idea of concerning the mandate of Turkey, but he said of course no one can say what the Council will think of tomorrow.

November 5th 1919. I thought of my poor Assyrian nation. They have suffered, they have been massacred and fought with the Allies, but we have no one championing our cause. Jews have money, Armenians have American people and Armenian English Committee and untiring Nubar Pasha Greeks her Venezelosi. I feel sorry when I see my inability to perform great things, then, on the other hand, when I notice among Assyrians denominential and personal feelings, my heart bleeds. I wish that I was able to show to the world and to the Allies that the Assyro-Chaldeans are the descendants of a great historic nation and still possess the qualities of that great nation, if given freedom and opportunity. For the achievment of such a result we must have a well organised bureau. Unfortunately we are lacking good, honest and sacrificing men. Assyrians must unite, casting aside the religious prejudices and join under one national flag.

November 6th 1919. Messrs. Radji and Ablahad are in Paris. I took these gentlemen first to the American Delegates. It was asked if the Assyrians speak their own language and I was asked if I could give them a brief statement concerning Assyro speaking Assyrians. *gave him necessary information.*

November 8th 1919. Escorted our delegates to see Mr. Werda. They insisted that all Assyrians must unite regardless the name. They have accepted the name of Assyro-Chaldean and they wish to work under that name. Talked of the question of sending some men to different places in Turkey, to have a conference at Constantinople etc.

November 10th 1919. Received an answer to my letter from Rev. Heazell regarding the arrival of Lady Surma - writing in the following way - "Lady Surma's arrival is the best thing that could have happened for the Assyrian nation, as she has been sent to England by the British Government. She has already been in treaty with the Foreign Office who listened to her with respects. So you can be comforted that everything that can be done is now being done." Tomorrow I am taking Dr. Yonan and Prof. Yohannan to an interview with the Archbishop of Canterbury & F.A.Heazell. Today I have received a letter from Adena, in which the director describes the endeavour of gathering the Orphans together who are begging in the streets and opening an Orphanage. This is a splendid work and I have recommended its continuance and asked immediate help from the Ex. Committee.

Severious Mutras Afram Barsoam during our conversation referred to his corpou ~~that, after~~ promising Patriarch to come to Paris, the people in America failed in their promise. Though his visit is ~~~~ it depends upon the financial assistance of A.N.A. I asked Mutras to call a meeting which he did.

After November 13th 1919. We had a Meeting at the Hotel Normandy. Mr. Werda and Mutras exchanged compliments. Mutras wished to know about our work during the past months to which we answered him.

November 16th 1919. Mutras accompanied by his brother and myself called upon Mr. Werda. After Severious Barsoam's departure, Mr. Werda made a remark on a charge which I cannot forget. He said "Your letters have done more damage, nearly splitting the Association" I leave this matter to the judgements of Ex. Committee. *and the Assyrians in America!*

At my advice, Mutras called a Meeting for November 31st 1919. Messrs. Radje and Abhalad were present. Mr. Werda was not present. We talked about united Assyrians, but they said as long as Chaldean brothers have adopted that name, as long as that name has been recognised officially, it is better to go on working under that name. We talked about establishing a bureau for which I have spoken so often and/return to America - about financial aspect taken into consideration. For the present to establish a national paper and try to organise or create a committee in London and in America. Severious Mutras Ofram Barsoam promised to prepare an Assyrian History etc.

November 22nd 1919. With Severious Mutras Afram Barsoam ~~with~~ visited Minister de Instruction Publique et de Bureau Arts, where we saw Mr. Lafferre, the purpose of this visit was to find out if there was a possibility of admitting some Assyrian young students into the University for higher education. He promised to see and arrange the matter with the Commission?

November 28th 1919. Visited the French Foreign Office - from there to the department of Asia.

November 29th 1919. *at the* British Delegation, where I was told about the treaty with French concerning Mesopotamia's division between the two Governments. This gave me the clue of writing a protest in our memorandum.

December 3rd 1919. Visited again department of Asia to see, *if Mr Gout* possible, Mr. Bartelot, plenipotencier. Saw his Sub-secretary, who gave me the idea of French occupying North of Mesopotamia.

December 6th 1919. I had another interview with the British Delegate explaining to him the vital issue of the Assyrian claims - that all Mesopotamia must come under one mandate. I have pointed out the necessity of its unity, then I tried to bring out the rightful claim of the Assyrians and the benefit to the mandatory power. Again talking about the people in Bakuba and Urmia about boundaries etc. He advised me to see Mr Hertjeal if I am in London also others, giving me a letter of introduction to Sir Hertjeal. He advised me to be in touch with French Foreign Affiars as the French Government is interested

in North East part of Mesopotamia. Mr. Said Radje showed me
a letter from Constantinople concerning the unfortunate affair
between Patriarch and some Members of the "ational Council.
I made an arrangement with the Metropole in regard to this
matter. In this Meeting we decided to send a Telegraph to
Patriarch and Messrs. Radje and Ablahad to Mr. Lutfi to go
and see the Patriarch at Metropole and Dr. Yoosuf will
telegraph to his beatitude in regard to your matter. I sent
a telegram to Patriarch under the date of December 8th 1919
"Stop accusations against the members of the National Council
for the sake of the nation" Rep. of Assyrians in America.
There are trouble makers in both parties, both among the
Chaldeans and Assyrians.

December 18th 1919. Rev. J. Y. Neesan *Naayan* organising a committee
for the relief of Chaldean Orphans. Lady Sykes is interested
in this committee.

I visited Mr. Carr one of the members of the Peace
Conference and he told me the arrangement for Mesopotamia.
The French and British zone of influence - evidently dividing
the country and the nation into two. I prepared a supplementary
memorandum in this regard.

December 21st 1919. With the Metropole visited His Excellency
Nubar Pacha. *mr Ablahad with us.* -

December 26th 1919. I sent a Telegram to the Prime Minister of
Great Britain and Lord Curzon, French Foreign Office, signed by Mr.
Radje, Metropole and myself. The Telegram read as follows:-

"The Turkish question is near its solution. Assyrian-Chaldeans
have suffered under misrule of Turkish government before the
war and during the war. Assyrians have fought for the cause
of Allied. Therefore we beg for the consideration of Assyrian
claims during the discussion of the Turkish question. We demand
justice, freedom and reparation for our sufferings and ask
an Assyrian free state under one mandatory power."

December 29th 1919. I received a letter from Adena signed by
Isa Savoni in which he informed me of a National Organisation
including all Chaldeans Assyrians. I answered him and encouraged
him for such an undertaking.

January 2nd 1920. At first Metropole did not wish to sign the
Supplementary Memorandum, but later on he consented to sign it.
After preparing a numerical statistic and a map, I delivered it
with the Memorandum to Mr. Kerr, Secretary to the Prime Minister,
Mr. Lloyd George and according to his wish, to other Delegates
and one to the Secretary of the Supreme Council. After talking
with Mr. Kerr, he referred me to see Messrs. Adams and Van Sinter.

January 13th 1920. I saw Mr. Van Sinter and talked to him about
the future of the Assyrians, the British attitude toward Assyrians,
British Government thinking about Assyrians. She wanted the same thing what
she acknowledges

her services given to the Allies and especially to England and
will surely consider our claims.

January 7th 1920. ~~Money affairs worrying Metropole. I gave him~~
~~some Frs. Mr. Ablahad is not financially fixed owing money.~~
~~I do not know how I can help all the Delegates. I have already~~
~~informed the Committee about Mr. Ablahad and Yacoboff.~~

January 9th 1920. Visited again Hotel Campbell, the Head Quarters
of the British Delegation, and saw Col. Gribbon. Mr. Montagu the
chief of the Indian Office is with the Delegates.

January 11th 1920. Passed all Sunday afternoon at Claridges Hotel
seeing some of the Delegates. I was told by Mr. Karr that the
English and French Governments have come to an understanding in
regard to Mesopotamia demanding again the numbers of Assyro-
Chaldeans in the region will be occupied by both the Governments.
Preparing the statistics and the Map I have delivered it to the
Secretary of the Prime Minister of Great Britain. He promised to
draw the attention of Mr. Lloyd George to the Supplementary
Memorandum of the Statistics (Jan. 13th 1920)

January 13th 1920. Visited Quai D'Orsay - French Foreign Minister's
Office. In these days both French and English Delegates were
not taking seriously the Kurdish question. However, he said it
was a difficult matter to settle the Turkish question with all its
many faces, nevertheless Assyro-Chaldeans claims are before the
Conference. One of the Delegates remarked that the whole world
fought against German Militarism, now the whole world must fight
to settle Oriental or Eastern Question. To carry on the terms of
the Treaty Powers must have force and men in Asia. I told them
it would be a folly to leave to Turkey the great part of the
territories again in his hands. She will never do what she promises
to do. Never show the capacity and the inclination to govern the
Christians rightly, giving them their freedom. Assyrians refused
either to become under Kurdish dominion or under Arabs' control.
Mr. Van Salter asked me to feel French sentiments in regard
to Mesopotamia.

January 14th 1920. All the day I tried to see Mr. Bartilot the
French plenipotencier. He is a busy man. The very afternoon I had
an interview with Mr. Montague, Secretary of the Indian Office?.
I had a talk with him expressing my thanks for the interest towards
Assyrians. He said the Peace Conference will arrange your affair.
I brought to his attention the matter of dividing the Mesopotamia
between the Governments of France and England. I protested against
such a precedence, pointing out the disadvantages of such a division
in preventing the national union.

I visited Hotel Claridges, where I met Mr. Roberts the head
of the direction of the Associated Press in Paris. I had a talk
with him in regard to the Syrian claims and I promised to contribute
something to the papers.

January 16th 1920.   Today I visited the Editor of the Temps -
Mr. Lemougain and he asked me to write a brief statement
and to give it to him, which I did.

January 17th 1920.   Visited Quai D'Orcy to see Mr. Bartilot and
I was ushered into the room of Mr. Begeton. He mentioned the
names of our colleagues - Messrs. Namuk and Najib and asked me
if I was in accord with their claims and if all Assyrians were
working together. I answered "Yes". He said, of course the
French Government cannot tell at present the arrangement
of the Peace Conference for the present French zone of influence
is from Syria until Diarbiker and the British around Mosul.
But I brought to his attention the demand of the Assyro-Chaldeans
of one mandate, not dividing the country. He continued and said
the French Government would look into the matter and come to an
understanding with the British Government.

From this Office I went direct to to Hotel Campbell, the
Head Quarters of the British Delegates, where I met the sub-
secretary Mr. G. Garbite with whom I had a long talk about our
claims. He began to say that there was not majority of Assyro-
Chaldean in any part of Mesopotamia. I told him of his mistake
and showed to him that he ought to take each element separate
and then he would find out the many places where the Assyrians
are in the majority. Of course at present you can expect
majority after massacres, deportation and immigration. He told
me the division among the Delegates - the Delegates from Urmi wants
the people to return there. Lady Surma wants his people to their
place. Chaldeans under French and you wish to have a place, a state
or a province for all. Naturally I argued his mistake - as all
wishing the freedom of Assyrians arround those sections that we
are demanding - all the Delegates agree on this point. Assyrians
do not wish to be divided, the only way to have a national existence
we demand one undivided Mesopotamia.

Two American Red Cross Officers visited Metropole ʌ Mr. *and myself*
Garwood and Major Bryson. They responded to our demand and heartily
wished to help Assyrians poor widows and Orphans.

Visited with the Metropole to American Red Cross Head
Quarters to see Col. Olds in this matter and he promised to do all
he could. He said he would send an urgent cable to Junior
Red Cross Society and hoped to hear a favourable answer.

January 18th 1920.   Corresponding with Lady Surma.

January 18th 1920.   Visited Chaldean Patriarch. His eminence
spoke very pathetically, expressing his extreme grief "My son, he
said, from Diaebiker as far as the gate of Masoul and hardly anyone
are left". "I presented to the French Government the same identical
claims like yours, but I have no hope now that the French Government
or the English Government will give us anything." *We must work to you.*

January 19th 1920. Today I was informed that the French will occupy
as far as Messinin and Ojile, but the exact boundary

has not been decided.

January 20th. 1920.   Visited again the American Red Cross Head-
Quarters, Rue de Chevreuse and had a talk with Colonel Olds, - *Olds*
Major Bryson and Dr.Garwood were present. Colonel Olds made the
following remarks :-

Firstly, he wanted to know the approximate amount of the need,
the number of the Orphans approximately, to which Metropole answered
1000 which I believe there are more I added.

Secondly, if the work would not interfere with the governing
power.

Thirdly, if the Red Cross would not interfere with the other
relief works - Col.Olds said he would send a cable to America in
regard to this matter. I thought surely this would help us in
both ways. First for our poor Orphans and Widows and Poor and
secondly, that it would be a good medium for the name of Assyrians.

January 21st. 1920. (Wednesday).   I had another interview with
Mr. Bergeton. He said if the French occupy that territory, the
French Government will give you "Autonomy" to govern your own affairs.
France will never be an Imperialistic Government. Speaking of the
reparation, he said the French Government will see to that and help the
Assyrians to build up the ruins, build schools etc., and help for
necessary things—for example, agricultural implements. The Assyro
Chaldean question has no direct relation with the Turkish Question,
but of course, it will come before the Conference.

January 26th. 1920.   Received a letter from Lady Surma expressing
her surprise at finding delegates from America. We spoke about
Lazar Yacohiff; Lady Surma has called him (Lazar Yacacoff) to London
but the English Authorities refused to Visa his Passport. Our question
will come in connection with the Turkish question within a few months.

January 27th. 1920.   Again visited the French Foreign Office.   It is
the same promise.

January 29th. 1920.   I was at the Office of "Le Temps" and had a talk
with the chief Editor in the Asiatic Department. He said there is no
majority of Assyrians in Mesopotamia - the arguments on both sides were
strong and heated, it is evident that "Le Temps" is pro-Turkish.
However, I gave him a statistic of my memorandum to study and write
something about it. The more I see the things the more I am convinced
of the necessity of establishing a Press Bureau; but "How?" That is the
great question for this alone needs a good organisation, money and men .
I am very very sorry that at the beginning our delegates could not agree
to work in harmony at least about such an important thing like this.
Newspapers do not care for individuals, all the information and the news
must come through the Bureau.   I am also strongly convinced that for
Propoganda work we must have a Bureau in London. We should have had t'
a few years ago, even after the Armistice.   I very much regret to tr'

to the attention of the Ex Committee that even in   America at the present time there is nå Assyrian Bureau for Publicity.

February 4th. 1920.   I called again at the American Red Cross
Quarters for news from America - have received no news ~~so far neither have I received any news from the Ex. Committee.~~

February 7th. 1920.   Left Paris for London and arrived at that place
at 8.0pm. Saturday and from there went to Waldorf Hotel where
Metropole is living.

February 8th. 1920.   I met Lady Surma at the Waldorf Hotel where
I met her formally. On Sunday morning I was introduced to Dr. Louis
Western Gambon, who is a lecturer on Tropical Medicine. He said he
will be glad to lecture on Mesopotamia, Assyria and her possibilities
"if you can organise a Committee." For this purpose I had a talk with
Metropole as I hoped to find out the old organisation and through
them, catry out a propoganda.

February 9th.,   I called upon Lady Surma at The Retreat where
I asked her about her work, her course in regard to the Assyrian
Question. I told her of our claims and demands in not dividing the
Mesopotamia. We demand the mandate of one power over Assyria
whether English or French. Her answer was that she perfectly
understood it all but would the Powers give us these things. The
question is on our part to demand our rights, although it is fulfillment
depends upon the will of the Peace Conference. If it meets we all
demand directly the mandate of the British Government Mar Shimoon
has asked the British Protection. I left a copy of the memorandum
with her. assuring that all the assyrians will be glad of English over the mandate of
all the Assyrians.

January 10th. 1920.   With Metropole I visited the Foreign Office
in the absence of Lord Curzon and had an interview with Sir Tilly,
Metropole naturally was the Spokesman but unfortunately he seemed
not very well versed on the Near East Question, or at least with the
Assyrian Question. After a great deal of talk he said that the
British Government will not go above Mosul and that we are not sure
at present about that part of the country. However, the Peace
Conference will look after the Assyrians.

February 11th. 1920.   The Indian Office does not think that
England will take the mandate of Mesopotamia - which means for the
Assyrian people - One of them suggested that why cannot Persia
be a mandatory power etc., the idea being this   since the Persian
Government is under the influence of the English ~~she will influence
the Assyrians also.~~ the Assyrians is better position

Lady Surma and Dr. Yonan are not on good terms.
I was informed that the British Government would send the people
somewhere near the British boundary in order that the Assyrians may be
protected. I have asked about the Dearbekir district this answer
was in the negative, also Hikiary and Bulamerg. I fall under a
great responsibility now than ever to I am informed that in
America the Assyrian Colony has the idea that the Assyrians had
their freedom and that the only dispute left is that of the boundaries.

200

which will be settled by the Supreme Council. I feel sorry
to see our people under such a false impression.

February 12th. 1920. At the Indian Office I saw Sir Wallace
Due and learned from this Office and definitely understood
that the Britishwill not go beyond Mosoul and they will not be
able to take the mandate of Mesopotamia. Then I asked what
would become of the Assyrians, and the answer was that the
Peace Conference would provide some way for your people.

January 13th. 1920. In accordance with my previous arrangement
I accompanied Metropole to see Mr. Allsthen Riley, 2 Kensington
Court. Sevirious Mutran Afram lead the conversation and
thanked him for his sympathy. We immediately plunged into
a conversation in regard to the organisation of a Committee
purely for the Assyrians, and reminded him of his previous
promise. He said he was afraid it would be difficult to
organise a committee as there are so many, but he advised
us to give a letter to the Archbishop of Canterbury in regard
to this matter.

February 14th. 1920. Received a letter from Dr. Halki in
Russia stating the terrible condition of those emmigrants whose
number exceeds over 25 - 30,000 people absolutely in a destitute
condition, asking me to do all I can for those people. I
have translated the letter,and the number of the families in
that region of Russia, and sent copies to many people including
the Lord Mayor of London and also to many leaders in the
Houses of Parliament. I have sent also 300 letters to the
members of the Houses of Parliament in regard to the Assyrian
question and appealed to them for assistance, also enclosing
in the communications the number of the massacred people
told them of the damage to our churches, monasteries, schools
etc., I have received letters from the leaders of the House.

February 15th. 1920. Visited again Lady Surma and again
asked her about her work etc., and again wanted her advice and
co-operation in our national cause - she said she was going
to do all she could for the Assyrians, and is furthering her
plans in regard to this work. The more I stay here or in
Paris the more I am convinced of the absolute necessity of
a Press Bureau for publicity. This is the only means by
which we can get near the hearts of the people . personal
work has no effect and the newspapers do not take much stocking
they only recognise a well organised bureau. Sorry we have
not and cannot have it under such a condition, when every
man is working for himself.
From the beginning we should have a body representing our
cause and through this channel should go every communication
and all information.

wish of Mr. Migran to see me.

tried to arrange a meeting for the three of us - Lady Surma,
Dr. Yonan and myself, and if possible Metropole also, but I
received no answer whatever.   Written another letter to
Lord Mayor's Secretary and another visé Count James Bryce.
In London there is a Committee going by the name of the
Armenian-British Committee, most of its members are from the
Houses of Parliament.   How can Assyrians organise such
a committee in such a time, under such circumstances.   How
is it possible to present our cause in a forceful way without
an organisation internal and external when the Assyrians on
the other side of the ocean do not realise the political
situation in Europe and the value of a great organisation.
<u>I repeat again the necessity of a Publicity Bureau!</u>

<u>February 24th. 1920.</u> I visited Sir Arthur Heartjel, in my
Interview I brought out the necessity of the Assyrian Union
under one mandatory power with necessary argument. He was
thoroughly convinced but he said the two powers have a secret
treaty in regard to the occupation of Mesopotamia. I told him
that the secret treaty was during the war time when they did not
know the outcome and then the circumstances were different
than today. To do this thing needs concession either by one or
the other Government. In answer he said my suggestion are correct
and he will bring these points to the attention of his colleague
adding do not worry of the outcome. We know about Assyrians much
more now than before.

<u>February 26th 1920.</u> At the House of Parliament.
<u>February 26th 1920.</u> I visited with the Metropole French Ambassador
Mr. Cambon.

<u>February 27th 1920.</u> We had an interview with the Daily Mail
reporter. Assyrian and Armenian Patrioreas are here.
Metropole and myself were invited to the reception of a committee
of Armenian given at the Hotel Carlton. There were representatives
from every nation and many members of the House of Parliament.
It has been a great propaganda for the cause of Armenia, where the
latest terrible massacre at Marash.

<u>February 28th 1920.</u> With the Metropole I visited the Bishop of
London R.C. R.H. Winnington Ingerham at Fulham Palace. In
reference to our request he said, but the ecclisastics have
not much influence upon the government as the most people think,
out; however; I will try to do all I can for your cause. We shall
have a meeting at Lamberth Palace when I will bring your question
forward.

<u>March 1st 1920.</u> I visited one of the leading and most influential
man in London - Bishop Gore . He was cordial but short in
his expression. He cannot do anything for Assyrians. I believe
the government will give to Nestorians some place.

Interest his Grace had shown for Nestorian Assyrian

Assyrians. Secondly I brought to his attention
there are Assyrians from other denominations. Thirdly
it is not justifiable to look after one part of Assyrians for
the sake of establishing a mission among them. Fourthly
Assyrians in Mesopotamia do not wish the division of that country
between two governments. Fifthly Assyrians demand an independent
State und[er] one Mandatory power. English or French.

March 3rd 1920. Interview with the "Empire" reporter, who
promised to make a Sunday Story. Metropole and myself present.

March 4th 1920. A great mass Meeting to protest against
the Turkey for the latest massacre at Marash. Viscount
Lord James Bryce presided. In his speech he spoke about
the sufferings of all the Christians in Turkey and the latest
massacre at Marash denouncing the action of Turkey.

I had the honour to meet Lord Bryce after the Meeting and
thanked him for championing the cause of suffering of the
Armenians and Assyrians. I sent him a letter a few days ago
and asked if I could send a list of *Assyrian massacres*.

march 6th 1920. With the Metropole I visited Lord James
Bryce, 3 Buckingham Gate. He was very cordial indeed and intereste[d],
knowing everything of Mesopotamia, the geography of Turkey.
He sympathised with the Assyro-Chaldeans' sufferings and their
fighting for the cause of democracy. He said, "I am sure
Turkey will not pass this side of the Taurus Mountains". He
promised to help our cause and speak at the Parliament. He
acknowledged my letter and said, after personal, I hope you do
not expect an answer to your letter.

I was told today by Mr. Nahoum that I had received four
hundred dollars and kept it for myself. Also he told me Mr.
Werda's statement in my regard to Metropole that Dr. Yoosuf
cannot be trusted. That I am causing the splitting up of the
..... That a terrible accusation. That a mean way of
injuring my reputation. .... understands me and others will.
I will appeal to the Assyrians *and judgment of Assyrians*.
I have written to America in truth and I hope the public will
understand the truth and judge me accordingly.

March 8th 1920. A letter to Mr. Asquith enclosing a supplementary
Memorandum of our damages. *London*

March 9th 1920. Mr. Bliss the treasurer of Armenian Relief
Committee called upon Metropole on my request. After talking
with him the advisability of having a Meeting at the Mansion
House. He expressed his fear that it would not be successful
as they have tried some notable speakers; but all have declined.
However, he said if I come to Victoria Street, the Head Quarters,
we may think it over.

... I saw there was no good will ... money ... questions were being raised. I asked how ... the ...nonian Relief Fund was exclusively for the Armenians. The answer was only 95%. Then I asked were the other 5% went and he said to other Christians in Turkey. On that ground I asked if the Assyrians were entitled to that 5%, which was never given to them at any time.

They promised to help the Assyrians, but there is a clause in their laws that all the funds would be distributed by an English agent, but at present there is none there, but may be the American Mission may help them or I suggested, through the Assyrian Patriarch and the Committee.

This matter was left for Mr. Bliss to arrange and I was obliged to take the initial step and ask them to send immediate help to the Assyrian Orphanage at Adana and the Committee sent a Telegram to Mr. Kennedy to this effect.

March 9th 1920. Messrs. Manik and Najib are in London. Our conversations and the methods of working in London. Firstly, that it will be in the same line as ours - Assyria - Chaldean without giving a religious aspect for which they answered the very same thing - that this is a national affair - they have nothing to do with the religion and they detest the idea of church in this vital question. They will *see* high Officials in order to effect *the* propaganda work, ~~......~~

work *London*

March 9th 1920. At the Church of St. Saviour, Southwark Mass Meeting was held for the Christians in Turkey; Metropole, from ...radan, ...nonian Patriarch or the Greek Archbishop being present. *where the speaker spoke of Assyro - Chaldeans.*

March 10th 1920. Called upon the secretary of Mr. Lloyd George.

March 12th 1920. A Meeting of Anglican Clergymen invited our Archbishop also, where there were some explanations in regard to Oriental Churches.

March 13th 1920. Again called at the Foreign Office to find out something definite about us, and was told that the Supreme Council will think of the Assyrians.

March 14th 1920. Sunday; there was an Open Air Meeting in the famous Trafalgar Square. The Meeting was to protest against letting the Turks stay at Constantinople, against the atrocities committed by Turks towards Christians - passed Resolutions - at that Meeting Dr. Yonan and myself spoke.

March 16th 1920. I was invited by the Lord Mayor of London to a luncheon at the Mansion House with Metropole. We were driven in State Carriages from the Guild Hall to the Mansion House. At

Bible House. These incidents and Meetings are nothing but propaganda.

Hire again I visited the House of Parliament and was glad
to hear the name of Assyria mentioned — in the House of Lords,
Lord James Bryce mentioned the Assyrian sacrifice and fighting and
asked the Government for Assyro-Chaldean rights.

March 17th 1920. Left London for Paris. I am glad to report
to the Honourable Committee that our endeavour in London has
been to bring among parliamentary circles, and clergy, our
existence and our claims, and have succeeded more or less.

Paris

March 18th 1920. Received American Red Cross Society expressing
their regret that they will not be able to do anything for
Assyrians in this section as Washington have not consented.
However, they promised to do something through Relief Committee.
March 20th 1920. Visited French Foreign Offices
March 26th 1920. Gave our respects with Metropole to Armenian
Catholicos from Sis.
March 31st 1920. It will not be out of the way to bring to the
attention of the Ex. Committee of Mr. Aram Ablahad. He is
here for a long time without money. His complaint has been the
finance has tied him down and he can do nothing. He demands
money to go to London. He says the Assyrians in America are
obliged to help him. I gave him a sum for his journey to London.
It is not a question of what he can accomplish but the fact that
he wants to go, *and he needs money*

The unfortunate thing again is the individual work and
the fact that he is not known.

March 26th 1920. Accompanied by Metropole I visited the
.... Mr. Berington repeated the
same statements that French Government will give autonomy to
Assyro-Chaldeans. France will treat her people equal regardless
of their religions differences.

Diarbeker Report though will be left under the
Turkish Suzerainty, but French influence will be there.

Mr. Ablahad asked for money from London. Correspondence
with Messrs. Malik and Najib in London, also Lady Surma and
Dr. Yonan.

April 14th 1920. I visited the bureau of the Education, and had
an interview with Mr. Hammaret the chief of the Educational
Departments in regard to finding some way of educating Assyrians
in French Universities.

I was referred to Mr. Albert Milhurid, because he said
the admission question depends upon the financial departments.
"Of course he would, we will be glad to admit this certain
young men to our institutions."

Received a letter from Mr. Ablahad suggesting that I send a Telegram to the President of the League of Nations. I have already told him that I have sent a letter to him which I read to him and also one to Sir Drummend, the Secretary of the League of Nations.

April 20th 1920. Left Paris for San Remo to join Messrs. Namik and Majib, arriving there April 20th. Stopped at hotel Royal where the British Prime Minister and others were living.

Our work was to see some gentlemen there and make our presence known to the members of the Supreme Council. Our presence is only a moral effect and trying to prove that Assyro-Chaldeans were following their rights and claims. I had a talk with Mr. Van Satter and Mr. Adams informing me that Assyro-Chaldeans will have autonomy - Of course our delegates are disappointed. Mr. Campbell, the Private Secretary of Lord Curzon, told me that today (April 24th) Assyro-Chaldeans were discussed.

I have seen nearly all the American and English Reporters and presented them to our Delegates. We are told again about autonomy. While talking with Mr. Roberts, the chief of Associated Press, said the Assyro-Chaldean question will be settled between the two governments Of course your question is comparatively small, but nevertheless it is in the Treaty Act.

Every Delegate is hustling. I am here and there to do my last endeavour for the recognition of our cause, before the final act in regard to Turkey's Treaty. I gave a letter personally to Prime Minister Lloyd George, with the knowledge of my colleagues - colleagues

Things are winding up and the Delegates are gradually parting.

April 26th 1920. Before leaving Royal Hotel, Mr. Forbes Adams called me in one of the side rooms and told me the decision of the Supreme Council. Dearbekir, Sigert and so forth will be left under the suzerainty of the Sultan - the Assyro-Chaldeans' rights will be protected. Beginning Beridjik, including Urfa, Mardin, Midiat Jizere, Nisibin, as far as the boundaries of Persia and from there a line drawn as far as Atul-Kemal will be under French with Autonomy. Of course for a few minutes I was amazed. I was surprised for such a decision, it was a blow for our existence, but what could I do but protest ? English will have from Zako to Mons-iliy etc. A commission will be sent to Constantinople in regard to the establishment of some form of Autonomy.

I left San Remo with Mr. Namik for Paris after a shortstop at Monte Carlo and Nice, arriving Paris on April 30th 1920. I noticed a pamphlet written in French about the massacre of Assyro-Chaldeans and their claims by Pere M. Kyriakas and Dr. V. Yonann, very similar to the one that was given by our colleagues.

May 3rd and 4th 1920. I visited British Delegation to find out the intention of British Government concerning the people of Salabe. While

Assyro-Chaldeans' place Autonomous, while ~~Nestorian~~ Assyrians *in Bakulah*
will be sent to their place if they wish - most probably between
Gawar and Ushan.

May 9th 1920. Trying to protest against the arrangement of the
Supreme Council for dividing the country into three or four
parts. I had an interview with the Editor of the Loeuvre in regard
to this matter.

May 10th 1920. To my question Lady Surma answered me as follows:-
"I do not know anything definite, but I have heard the Supreme
Council will send an international commission to ~~Kurdistan~~" *Kurdistan*

May 11th 1920. Present at Quai D'Orsay when the Allied handed the
Treaty Terms to Turkish Delegates. Immediately after the ceremony
I hustled again to the Office of Mr. Bergeton. He said "France
will have that part of the country and will give Autonomy Dearbekt
Harpoot Malatia, Sigert though under the Sultan's suzerainty, but
it will be French influence - Kurdistan will have local Autonomy"
decided by the International Commission. The Nestorian Assyrians
probably will be sent to their homes, it is much better for the
Assyrians-Chaldeans to increase the population in this region
where there is better chance of facilities than in those mountain
regions.

May 13th 1920. There is still another project said one of the
British Delegates. As far as Assyro-Chaldeans are concerned in
Mosul they are safe. The people of Bakuba will go to their place.
Of course it will be another boundary line giving Ushnu to Persia.
So the Assyrians will be nominally under Persia, but British
influence.

May 18th 1920. I received a letter from Dr. J. Yonan, London.
If we all appeal and ask from the British Government the place which
British Government has accepted - this is his scheme -

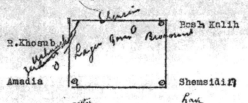

Of course this is a *neither* good scheme and I *have* answered his letter,
asking him if the British Government would officially give us this
place and under what conditions will she guarantee our safe-guard.
Will she be mandate and how will the people be able to go to
that place without home, without necessary agricultural implements
and many other vital questions, before deciding to go there. *We must
know the English promise, with many ns, matters to.*

agricultural implements and many other vital questions before
deciding to go there. If she is going to send the people of
Bakuba then, of course, our asking will not be of any use.
This is a good project for our cause in regard to the French
Government influence in North of Mesopotamia. No letter from
Dr. Yonan or Lady Surma in regard Dr. Yonan's scheme.

May 28th 1920. Mr. Namik and myself visited the French Foreign Office again. We were told the same thing - that France will
give Assyro-Chaldeans autonomy. French Government officially
will declare this after the signing of the Turkish Treaty
and see some of the other matters. Of course, I brought out
this scheme of the British. He immediately said:"how can
British Government all by herself a place inside of Kurdulan?"
adding: "if your people likes to go to the mountain regardless
of the advantages."

After all these things , there are two men here - as a
delegate Assyrians, who are really a burden upon my shoulders -
Both have no money and there is no chance for earning money.
Mr. Ablahad from Constantinople who claims that Assyrians in
America are bound to help him as he has some letters from
America, and second he cannot go to Constantinople, the other
Lazar Yacohoff, whose letters I have sent to the Ex Committee.
I have helped both as much as I could, and they are still not
satisfied and even hhreatened by Mr. Yacohoff to kill me.

Another thing which your representative was worrying
about was some letters from Armenia making all kinds of
suggestions some times with abuses but always complaining
why the newspapers did not write about Assyrians. The answer
is that the Assyrians have not a press bureau.

June 3rd 1920. I received a letter from Dr. Yonan in regard
to his scheme, who writes no definite news from British Government. I answered him again. up to this day,
(July 2nd 1920) there was no news.

June 10th 1920. A letter from Lady Surma in which she writes
"British Government has repatriated the people of Bakuba to
the Vilayet of Masoul - they mean to settle them east of
Gawar to Ushnu and give them guns to defend themselves."

June 16th 1920. I sent a letter to Lady Surma concerning a
letter from Bakuba published in Izgada - no answer (July 2nd)

June 25th 1920. I wrote a letter to the Internation Red
Cross Section addressed to Major W.R. Bereford for the
recognitions of Assyro-Chaldeans nation.

July 5th 1920. My life is threatened by Mr. Yacohoff and
I am helpless. I have done all I can for him ans still he
prosecutes me. He follows me every where I go and watch me
no outside of my hotel. I have written to the Ex Committee
in regard to Yacohoff and Mr. Ablahad - no answer yet. It
is a terrible existance indeed. If I am killed for the

208

nation's welfare I am satisfied but I do not like to be a
victim of a man who has no conscience and no respect for any
body person .

July 5th 1920. The Supreme Council has arranged the affairs
of Turkey. To solve the Turkish question Italy must fight
with Greece (which she is unwilling to do and averse to helping
Turkey secretaly) British and French will have to reduce
Arabs, then there is some possibility of rest. Even now while
the Allies are temporarily occupied, difficulties are arising.
The Arab has refused to accept the decision of the European
Council. Turks and Arabs will fight, how and for how long
is the question. The only salvation of Christians and the
settlement of the Near East question should be by the American
Government. She has refused to do it and the near east
remains exactly as grave and menacing a problem as ever.

July 6th 1920. A letter from Lady Surma stating that she is
not responsible if the Allies did not give what the Assyrians
demanded . She has done all she could in the circumstances.
The power is not in her hands, then she recites the humber
of the delegates who have worked independently from her
referring to Dr. Yonan and Mr. Lazar Yacokoff and Chaldians.

July 15.- Our national fate has a great deal to do with the French Success in Syria, and when the Arab question is settled by the French, then it will facilitate the work of the French army to move up to that part of Mesopotamia, which french Government will be a mandatory power there.

July 24.- I have visited department of Asia and had a talk with his Excellancy Mr Bergeton who said the things are better in Syria, hope later on our army will move on further; promising the same thing again then I asked him if he will give me an official letter for America to present it to our people" he said yes"

July 27.- Visited Mr Bergeton not there

July 28.- On this promise I visited him again with Mr Namik again repeated his promise but he said he cannot give that letter immediate-ly for some reasons known to him . He said, however that if you are in hurry to go to America he will send that letter later on, he entered in to some questions evedently not believing or at least not showing his con-fidence in the matter of our union.- our national union for example he asked have you a national union like Armenians - ask if there is any Asayro -Chaldean Central Committee to these questions I have answered in some way that he convinced the existence of some organization, Armenians have one two delegates only etc...

July 28.- I am sorry to hear unpleasant things about the A.N.A., and the argument of some branches in regard of the President and Mr Rev You Allah coming to Paris, threatening that if they are not send to Paris they will leave off the membership of the A.N.A.; as far as my per-sonal conviction concerns- it is a poor argument and a poor attitude

" As for working only for Turkish Assyrians"

I beg to differ with those gentlemen, as I will proove that, we have
considered the whole Assyro-Chaldean affair more carefully and I
have helped to Lazar Yacaboff for the last year.

July 28.- Written a letter to Patrick *E*lias III in regard for
Assyro- Chaldean organization and his duty toward that organization
to recognize it and help it, a letter to Mr Radji also. I have
answered to Mr Dartly's suggestion in regard of sending some one
from here to America:-

August 3.- I gave a letter to Mr Bergeton, in regard to his promise,
in Mr Bergeton's absence I gave it to Mr Depera who promised to look
to this matter, as he says he realizes the situation, and inform me

Aug 3.- To day we had some informal talk among three of *us*. Messrs
Hemak, Abdahad and myself - it was decided sending letters to Constantinople for the union of Assyro-Chaldeans and organize a central committee for a future congres.

Glad to hear the peace between, Patriarch and National Council, I
feel satisfied playing my roll in regard this matter; after all
Patriarch has come to an understanding. *treaty*

Aug 10.- after all the Turkish, *was* signed- none of our question, is *how*
left with the French Governement, I have not received any answer
for my letter as yet, I will wait few days before going to *the* Department
of Asia, I will not keep quiete until I receive a definite official
answer.

12

Aug Visited to day department of Asia, I had a long talk and
some hot arguments in regard Assyro Chaldian situation, and the
French attitude toward the recognition of Assyro Chaldian Autonomy.-

In reply he said after having Conférehce with the cheifs of this
bureau " have decided that it is too early yet to give you such a
letter of promise as the treaty has been signed only few days
ago - and it will take some time to settle the affairs there.-
however he said the "French mandate is certain and the Government
is ready to give every thing and every facility for their progress"
he argued that there are not many assyro - Chaldeans there, but
in reply said to him our massacre until later days and our deportation - the people will return to this place when they are sure
of French mendate and Assyro Chaldean Autonomy" he said it will
be given to the people to that promised autonomy but he cannot
give an official letter just now. I asked him when? answered
when every thing is settled reminding me to present Polish- Soviet
Conflict.repeating again - Let Your people be sure of French
mendate and of her promise:

Aug 24 - 1920. I had a talk again with Mr Bergiton
who repeated the promise of the government, hoping the
French will soon occupy the territory. And the things - what
you have to do he said - to be ready to occupy this
region with your people. when the time comes the
French government will give all the facilities for trans
portation, He asked me. where is the best place
for the central government in Mardin or Ourfa.
to which I have answered ourfa - being the ancient
called for Assirian Empire. the things are better he ca
hope we soon establish a government like Lebanon etc
Aug 30. American Relief Committee is helping our Orphanage at Adana
ob my frequent request, stating the disasters

Sett, - A letter to foreign offices of British government.
Assyrians at Bakuba, & the attitude of the British government.

Permit me to present to the Executive Committee the following
suggestions, for our national Cause

1°.- The Assyrian nation as a whole was not ready and prepared
to grasp the omportance of such a great problem.

2°.- Lack of a national organization in Turkey or in America
founded on a sound principles including every
elements;

3°.- Lack of a National Treasury

4°.- Unsuccesfull attempt in presenting Assyrian Cause

(a) having not a recognized Body of delegates.

(b) no means of an extensive work for propaganda in Europe
or in America for the cause of our liberty, and our sufferings

(c) no unity among the delegates in presenting our claims by
a recognized body in aproper way.

5°.- Lack of establishing an Assyro -Chaldean bureau of publication.

6°.- Lack of head quarter in Paris.

WHAT WE NEED AT PRESENT ANS WHAT WILL BE OUR WORK
FOR THE FUTURE

1°.- A well organized Assyro-Chaldean National Union. whose purpos
will be purely national, no religious or sectarrensym must enter
in this union.

2°.- Word The immediate need of a press bureau.

3°.- A central Assyro& Chaldean Committee some where in Turkey...

4°.- A national Treasury for the present and for the future use

(a) ~~for~~ look after educational work

(b) to furnish necessary funds for agricultural impliments

for homes etc

(c) to help the people for establishing business corporation ~~ets~~

(d) to en courage the Assyrians- Chaldians to go to this new home

(e) ~~to~~ propoganda work

4°.- To interest the capitalists in this part of the country.

5°.- To organize Relief work

6°.- A newspaper (national organ)

7°.- If possible to organize a congress from different parts

in Turkey, in Persia, Russia India America in a neutral Country-

like Switzerland. ~~this is flousible if the french government~~

~~do what we ask to her after propose~~

Sept. 10 - 10.30. A.M. Visited Foreign office once more to give
my respect to Mr Bargeton. He assured me that French government
will fullfill his promise, and this is not very far - at the
things are going on very nicely in Cilicia and Syria - Take the
massage to your people that French government will give
autonomy to Assyro- Chaldean. He said within a short time and
he will give that authorized letters to Mr Namik - and
a copy to you."

Sept. 20 -1920

Yours Respectfully
foreign
Rep. of Assyrians "

PART VII

EXTRACTS

Yoosuf Abraham K, student, 829 n Howard
Yorgt Geo T, uphlstr, Loney la
York Adam, lab, Brooklyn, A A Co
York Barbara Mrs, 1711 e Chase
*York Club (The), 10 w York
*York Geo A, canmkr, 1228 n Gay
York Jeannette Mrs, 917 n Caroline
York John B, cigarmkr, 1618 n Bethel
*York John W, lab, 730 Stirling
*York Jos, lab, 258 Chesnut
York Mnfg Co, ice, 620 Buren
YORK RIVER LINE, Ticket Office, 205 e Balto (see advt)
York Road Ry, tee City and Suburban Ry Co
York Road Real Estate Office, Augustus D Clemens Jr, Hoen Bldg, 306 e Lexington
York Southern Ry, John S Bull, frt and passenger agt, 53 Central Savings Bank Bldg
*York Wm J, lab, 258 Chesnut
*Yorker John W, waiter, 911 Linden av
*Yorkman Nancy, laund, 907 Stirling
*Yorkman Isaac, lab, 231 n Durham
*Yorkman Saml C, lab, 231 n Durham
*Yorkman Wm J, canmkr, 1722 e Fayette
Yorzcrinski Peter, lab, 600 s Ann
Yospy Jos, tailor, 724 s Charles
Yost Andw, harnessmkr, 1507 Pa av
Yost Annie B Mrs, 429 w 23d n
Yost Annie F, hairdresser, 1026 McDonogh
Yost Cath, dressmkr, 1428 Aisquith
Yost Chas, brushmkr, 118 Leloup
Yost Chas J, baker, 2711 Pa av
Yost Conrad, salesman, 122 n Dallas
Yost Conrad jr, lab, 606 s Castle
Yost Danl, lab, 624 s Bradford
Yost Ella, 406 King
Yost Geo, brasswkr, 1026 McDonogh
Yost Geo, instmkr, 927 Milton pl
Yost Geo, mach, 927 Milton pl
Yost Henry, barber, 21 w Pratt
Yost Henry, fireman, 1735 n Patterson-pk av

Yost Jacob, lab, 606 s Castle
Yost Jacob, lab, 3034 Fountain
Yost Jacob, lab, 1362 Towson
Yost John, cabtmkr, 1428 Aisquith
Yost John, clk, 1026 McDonogh
Yost John jr, clk, 1428 Aisquith
Yost John C, varnisher, 302 n Stricker
Yost Lilly A, bkpr, 1428 Aisquith
Yost Louisa, saleslady, 1428 Aisquith
Yost Richd D, 1231 Argyle av
Yost Wilhelmina, seamstress, 1428 Aisquith
Yost Wm F, bkpr, 416 Mosher
Yost Wm F, steamfitter, 1164 Cleveland
Yost Wm J B, bkpr, 1428 Aisquith
Yost Wm McL, physician, 1231 Argyle av
Yost Wm O, agt, 806 Ensor
Yot Lee, laund, 848 Hampson
You Hing, laund, 232 Park av
You Kee, laund, 1501 Myrtle av
You Know Pleasure Club, 28 Harford rd
Youck Florence, dressmkr, 416 Roland av
Youmans Chas, salesman, 269 Rogers av
Youmans David D, salesman, 269 Rogers av
Youmans Geo F, student, 1023 McCulloh
Young A Klotz, collector, 1138 Highland av
*Young Absalom, lab, 615 Raborg

Young Ada Mrs, 5 Fairview av
Young Adam, grocer, 515 n Central av
*Young Albert, lab, 237 State
*Young Albert, porter, 1370 n Fremont av
Young Albert B, pilot, 1433 Riverside av
Young Aldridge, mnfs agt, 497 Exchange pl, h 5 e Franklin
Young Alex (Young, Creighton & Diggs), 630 w North av
Young Alex, lab, 1826 Byrd
*Young Alfred, driver, 231 Herring ct
Young Alfred, porter, 1723 Maccubbin
Young Alfred A, insp, 11 Penn
*Young Alfred H, mess, 626 n Eutaw
Young Alice H, nurse, 21 n Carey
Young Alphonsus J, clk, 1110 Ashland av
*Young Alvin H, lab, 925 n Woodyear
*Young Amy, laund, 511 Jasper
*Young Anderson, lab, 341 w mans
Young Andw, paver, 311 n Amity
Young Andw J, clk, 539 n Fulton av
*Young Anita, 822 China
*Young Annie Mrs, 325 w Lombard
Young Annie Mrs, 6 w North av
Young Annie E, nurse, 150 w Lafayette av
Young Annie L, opr, 220 Carroll a
Young Annie R Mrs, 1521 Kensett
Young Anton, tailor, 222 Parkin
*Young Arthur, lab, 731 Church n w
Young Arthur J, bkpr, 1731 e Eager
Young Arthur M, carp, 1731 e Eager
Young Barbara Mrs, 308 s Chester
Young Barbara Mrs, 248 Sycamore av
*Young Benj, lab, 293 Dawson al
*Young Benj, lab, 1407 Tenfoot al
Young Bertha C, seamstress, 2144 Wilkens av
Young Blanche M, dressmkr, 33 s Carey
*Young Boniface J, lab, Garrison av
Young C Cooper, clk, 1700 Edmondson av
Young C Grifith, supt White-Crosby Co, h 301 e Mt Royal av
Young Calvin, lab, 621 Wayne
Young Caroline Mrs, 15 n Washington
Young Caroline Mrs, 2144 Wilkens av
Young Carrie, stenog, 401 e 24th n
Young Carrington A, 1022 n Fulton av
Young Casper, shoemkr, 806 s Bdway
*Young Cath, dressmkr, 134 Rogers av
Young Cath, grocer, 205 n Amity
Young Cath, laund, 8 Rabe av
Young Cath Mrs, 1122 Argyle av
Young Cath M Mrs, 833 n Gilmor
Young Celia Mrs, 317 s Caroline
Young Central Pleasure Club (The), 117 s Central av
*Young Chas, butcher, 2216 Etting
Young Chas, coal, 701 w Barre
Young Chas, foreman, 2133 e North av
*Young Chas, lab, 906 n Howard
*Young Chas, lab, 917 Peach al
*Young Chas, lab, 311 n Pine
Young Chas, oysters, 900 Claret al, h 997 Russell
Young Chas, stonectr, 2219 Jefferson pl
Young Chas A, distiller, 1110 w Hamburg
Young Chas A, mariner, 1433 Johnson
Young Chas C, molder, 1009 Ashland av
Young Chas D, printer, 1303 Hollins
Young Chas E, clk, Ry M S, p o
Young Chas E Rev, 1905 Harlem av
Young Chas E, varnisher, 652 w Saratoga
Young Chas F, cabtmkr, 1814 w Pratt
*Young Chas F, saloon, 2135 e North av
Young Chas H, carp, 3510 Bruce ter
*Young Chas H, driver, 208 s Bethel
Young Chas M, turner, 6 Pleasant
Young Chas W, canmkr, 511 e Fort av
Young Chas W, lab, 1306 Pa av
*Young Christian, tinner, 1048 James al
*Young Clarence, porter, 1322 Whatcoat
Young Clark, lab, 12 Montebello av
Young Conrad, electrician, 2212 Orleans
Young Conrad, florist, 1501 Hopkins av e

As a medical student, Dr. A. K. Yoosuf lived in Baltimore, MD. He is listed on the very top of the left column in this Baltimore city directory for 1895.

The New Assyria.

FULL REPORT OF THE

FOURTH ANNUAL CONVENTION

OF THE

ASSYRIAN NATIONAL ASSOCIATIONS

OF AMERICA

HELD AT

New Britain, Connecticut

December 18, 19 and 20

1 9 1 9

Cover page of the convention report.

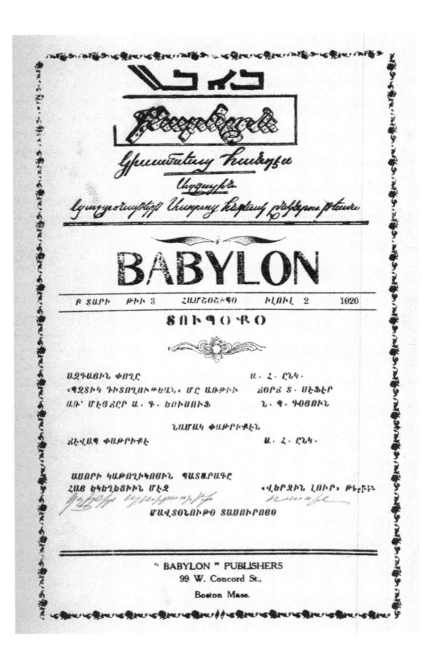

Cover page of *Babylon*.

62332

[Edition of August, 1914.]

[FORM FOR NATURALIZED CITIZEN.]

FEB 7 1919

DIVISION OF
PASSPORT CONT...
JAN 23 1919
DEPARTMEN...
OF STATE

UNITED STATES OF AMERICA,

STATE OF *Mass*

COUNTY OF *Worcester*

I, *Abraham K. Yoosuf, Capt. M. C. FEU*, a NATURALIZED AND LOYAL CITIZEN OF THE UNITED STATES, hereby apply to the Department ... Washington, for a passport.

I solemnly swear that I was born at *Harpoot, Asia* on *the date of Dec 17 – 1866* .... ; that my father, *Kevork Yoosuf* (Name) was born in *Harpoot, Asia* (Country) and is now residing at .... that I emigrated to the United States, sailing from *Liverpool, England* about *Nov., 1889*, ... ; that I resided *36* years, uninterruptedly, in the United States, from *1889* to *1919* at *Baltimore ... practising in Worcester*; that I was naturalized as a citizen of the United States before the *Superior* Court of *Mass* at *Worcester, Mass* on the *12th of Jul*, 1896, as shown by the Certificate of Naturalization presented herewith; that I am the IDENTICAL PERSON described in said Certificate; that I have resided outside the United States since my naturalization at the following places for the following periods:

Surgeon in Balkan w..., from *1912 Jul* to *1913 Sept.*
Surgeon at Board w..., from *1914 July* to *1915 Dec.*

and that I am domiciled in the United States, my permanent residence being at *Worcester* in the State of *Mass*, where I follow the occupation of *Physician*.

My last passport was obtained from *Department State of Washington No 68408* on *March 30th 1912* and was *Still ...* I am about to go abroad temporarily, and intend to return to the United States within *a year* [months / years] with the purpose of residing and performing the duties of citizenship therein; and I desire a passport for use in visiting the countries hereinafter named for the following purpose:

England & France (Name of country.)
.... (Name of country.)
.... (Name of country.)

I intend to leave the United States from the port of *New York* (Port of departure.)

sailing on board the *unknown* (Name of vessel.) on or about *Feb. 1st, 1919*

FEE
DETACHED

OATH OF ALLEGIANCE.

Further, I do solemnly swear that I will support and defend the Constitution of the United States against all enemies, foreign and domestic; that I will bear true faith and allegiance to the same; and that I take this obligation freely, without any mental reservation or purpose of evasion: So help me God.

Abraham K. Yoosuf, C.H. M.C.
(Signature of applicant.)

Sworn to before me this *15th* day

of *January* 19*19*

JAN 30 1919

W. J. Hopkins

Asst Clerk of the Superior Court at Worcester Mass

[OVER.]

JAN 23 1919

Dr. A.K. Yoosuf passport application as of January 15th 1919. (Page 1 of 3.)

Age: *5 3* years.

Stature: *5* feet, *6½* inches, Eng.

Forehead: *Medium High*

Eyes: *Brown*

Nose: *Prominent*

Mouth: *Medium*

Chin: *Full*

Hair: *Dark & Grey*

Complexion: *Dark Swarthy,*

Face: *Rather Square*

Distinguishing marks: _____

IDENTIFICATION.

January 15th, 19*19*

I, *T. S. Johnson* _____, solemnly swear that I am a {native} {naturalized} citizen of the United States; that I reside at *Worcester. Mass* _____; that I have known the above-named *Abraham K. Yoosuf* _____ personally for *8* ____ years and know {him} {her} to be the identical person referred to in the within-described certificate of naturalization; and that the facts stated in {his} {her} affidavit are true to the best of my knowledge and belief.

T. S. Johnson

Lawyer and Clerk of Court. Worn (Occupation.)

Worcester massachusett (Address of witness.)

Sworn to before me this ___*15th*___ day

of *January* _____, 19*19*

[SEAL.]

W. H. Hopkins

Asst Clerk of the *Superior* Court at *Worcester Mass*

Applicant desires passport to be sent to the following address:

Abraham K. Yoosuf. Capt. M.C.
92 Austin St.
Worcester, Mass *M.C.*

A signed duplicate of the photograph to be attached hereto must be sent to the Department with the application, to be affixed to the passport with an impression of the Department's seal.

Dr. A.K. Yoosuf passport application as of January 15th 1919. (Page 2 of 3.)

New York City, N. Y., January 17, 1919.

Dr. A. K. Yoosuf,

　　Worcester, Mass.

Dear Dr. Yoosuf:

　　In a regular meeting of the Executive Committee of the
Assyrian National Associations you were unanimously elected as
one of the delegates to represent the Assyrian nation at the
Peace Conference. We trust, therefore, you will be able to accompany the president of the National Associations to this patriotic
mission. We are fully aware of your patriotism, intellectual ability, efficiency, and familiarity with diplomatic etiquette.

　　　　　　　　　Sincerely yours,

　　　　　　　　　Charles S. Dartly, Secretary

　　Assyrian National Associations of America.

Further, I do solemnly swear that I will support and defend the Constitution of the United States
against all enemies, foreign and domestic; that I will bear true faith and allegiance to the same; and
that I take this obligation freely, without any mental reservation or purpose of evasion: So help me God.

　　　　　　　　　Leonard Yophrus Duly (Signature of applicant.)

Sworn to before me this __31st__ day

of __January__ 19 19

　　　　　　　　　Harry F. Rab　　FEB 3 1919

Deputy Clerk of the __U.S. Dist.__ Court at __Cincinnati, O.__

* A person born in the United States should submit a birth certificate with his application, or if the birth was
not officially recorded, affidavits from the attending physician, parents, or other persons having actual knowledge
of the birth.
† If the applicant's father was born in this country, lines should be drawn through the blanks in brackets.
[ovsn.]

54271

Dr. A.K. Yoosuf passport application as of January 15th 1919. (Page
3 of 3.)

NINEVEH

A MONTHLY PUBLICATION

DEVOTED TO THE ASSYRIAN PEOPLE

Published by The Assyrian Progressive Association

VOL. I, No. 12   BOSTON, MASS.   DECEMBER 1, 1927

ՆԻՆՈՒԷ

Կը հրատարակուի ամէն ամսուն 1-ին
Տարեկան բաժնեգինն է $3·00
վեց ամսուան համար $2·00
Չհաֆէ իրաքանչիւր օրինակ 30 սէնթ

Դրկուած ձեռագիրները հա չեն դարձուիր

67 School St., Everett, Mass.

Cover page of *Nineveh*.

APPENDIX

The Independence of Assyria[127]

By Said B. Shamsie, of England
Who is interested in the Assyrian National Cause

ONE: THE HISTORICAL CLAIM

The claims of Assyria to a recognition of her national unity are peculiarly strong. They are based alike on ancient history and traditions, on her Christianity, and on justice.

First let us glance at her history. Among all the manifold achievements of the last century few will bear comparison with the recovery and the decipherment of the monuments of ancient Nineveh. For centuries the great city had been buried beneath its own ruins – its history lost, and its very site forgotten. Even in the age of the classical writers of Greece and Rome it had passed into the region of myth. Ninos, or Nineveh, had become a hero-king of legend, whose conquests were supposed to have extended from the Mediterranean to India. Little but the account presented in the Old Testament was known of the mighty Assyrian Empire, and that little was involved in obscurity and doubt. Even the boldest dared not suggest that, buried beneath the ground lay the history of that splendid fabric ready to come to life again at the touch of the magician's wand. One by one the cuneiform characters were deciphered, and the message they concealed, was read, until, at last, it is possible to translate an

127. Source: *The New Assyria*, Vol. 3, No. 33, May 15 1919, pp. 1–7, 11. (*Editor*)

ordinary Assyrian text as certainly as a page of the Old Testament.

Revelations of the Ruins

The ruins of Nineveh yielded not only sculpture and inscriptions carved in stone, but also whole library of books. It is true they were written on clay and not on paper, but they are none the less real books, and the revelations they make are startling in the extreme. They deal with all the branches of knowledge in existence at the time, and give us a true and clear picture of Assyrian life and thought. It is strange to examine for the first time one of the clay tablets of the old Assyrian library. Usually it has been more or less broken by the catastrophe of that terrible day when Nineveh was captured by its enemies, and the palace and library destroyed together. But whether it is a fragment or a complete tablet, it is impossible not to handle it reverently when cleaning from it the soil with which its long sojourn in the earth has encrusted it, and spelling out its words for the first time for more than 2,000 years. When its last reader laid it aside, Judah had not as yet undergone the chastisement of the Babylonian exile, the Old Testament was an uncompleted volume, the Kingdom of Messiah a promise of the distant future. We are brought face to face, as it were, with men who were the contemporaries of Isaiah, of Hezakiah, of Ahaz; nay, of men whose names have been familiar to us since we first read the Bible by our mother's side, Abraham, Isaac and Jacob.

Important Discoveries

One of the most important results of these discoveries is the unexpected confirmation they afford of the accuracy of Holy writ. The latter part of the Old Testament history no longer stands alone. Classical history and legend afforded no confirmation of the sacred story, but the Assyrian records have completed the gap. The monuments of ancient Assyria have furnished us with records whose authenticity none can deny, which, read side by side with the Books of Kings, confirm, explain, and illustrate them in many details. The very language of the inscriptions has helped to explain many difficult passages of the Hebrew Bible. Assyrian proves to be closely related to Hebrew, the likeness being as close as that between two strongly marked English dialects.

The inhabitants of Assyria belonged to a Semitic stock; that is, they were allied to the Hebrews in blood and language. This receives confirmation from the Biblical table of nations (Gen x., 22), where the nation of Ashur is placed second among the descendants of Shem. The striking likeness of the Assyrian to the Hebrew type of face would, apart from the language, have sufficed to place this relationship beyond doubt. This kinship goes deeper, however, and asserts itself in certain clearly-marked spiritual tendencies, which find their expression in the national religions. Like their Hebrew brethren, they reached the conception of Divine unity at an early date. They acknowledged one supreme God and Master, and Him they called Ashur. The very expressions used in the two languages approximate in a remarkable way. The well-known phrase, "The Lord rained upon Sodom and upon Gomorrah brimstone and fire from the Lord out of heaven," has a close parallel in the Assyrian hymn which, in exact conformity to the Hebrew phrase, speaks of "raining stones and fire upon the foe." Similarly the Hebrew phrase, "the Lord of Hosts" finds its analogue in the common Assyrian title of the supreme God, Ashur. Accounts of the creation in six days, the Deluge, and the Tower of Babel, all closely agreeing with the Hebrew accounts, are found in the library of Nineveh.

Biblical History

It is in the domain of Biblical history that the light cast by Assyrian research has been clearest and strongest. For an example of the marvellous corroboration and illustration of Holy Writ afforded by them, it is only necessary to turn to the records of the monuments, and compare them with the contemporary narratives of the Books of Kings. The Bible informs us why Sennacherib left Hezekiah unpunished, and never despatched another army to Palestine. The cuneiform annals explain the reason of his murder, and why his sons fled to Ararat or Armenia. The single passage in the Scriptures referring to Sargon no longer remains isolated and unintelligible. We now know that he was one of the most powerful of the Assyrian conquerors, and we have his own independent account of the siege and capture of Ashdod.

Between the history of the monuments and Bible story is in strict harmony with the other. The monuments have proved to be the complement of much of the Old Testament, and the achievement of Assyria in this field of knowledge makes its claim upon us very real one. Some of the most important of these are the monuments of Shalmanesser II, whose military success exceeded even those of his father. His annals are chiefly to be found engraved on three monuments now in the British Museum. One of these is a monolith found at Kurkh, a place only 20 miles from Diyarbakir – my own home. The full-length figure of Shalmanesser is sculptured upon it, and the surface of the stone is covered with the inscription. With this brief account of ancient Assyria, I will pass on in a second article to a mention of the Assyrian Church and Christian times.

TWO: THE HISTORICAL CLAIM

The Assyrian Christians of Mesopotamia are the members of the Church of Antioch. In reviewing the history of this ancient Church we are brought face to face with Apostolic times. The Church of Antioch has claimed, and competent historians deem rightly, that she was founded by St. Peter, who became her first Bishop or Patriarch. Thus Dean Stanley, in his "Eastern Church," says the Church of Antioch is the oldest of all Gentile Churches. At Antioch the name of "Christians" was first used (Acts 11, 26). Among its famous sons, in the age of persecution, it produced Ignatius, and, in the age of the Empire John Chrysostom and John of Damascus. As to the claim of Antioch to be founded by St. Peter, he says, "the Eastern Church has often regarded itself as possessing whatever privileges can be claimed by the See of Rome on the ground of descent from the first Apostle." Another name by which the Church of Antioch is known is that of Jacobite. Many reasons are given to explain the origin of this name, one being that they are descended from Jacob or Israel, and another that they are the descendants of the earliest converts of St. James the Apostle. But there is yet a third reason, and this seems to be the more likely, namely, that they represent the followers of a certain Jacob Baradaeus, a monk and presbyter who lived in the 6th Century. Wandering disguised throughout the provinces he placed and established the Church upon a stronger basis. After he was made Bishop of Edessa he was better able to uplift the oppressed Church, and he ordained many presbyters over them. He remained thus for

33 years, when he died in A. D. 558. He found the Church oppressed, persecuted, and small; he left it flourishing and active.

It is unnecessary to follow the course of this Church down to the present day. I would only draw a comparison between the Church as she is presented to us in early times, and the sad picture she presents in the 20th Century. And in doing so what better example of her early life could I produce than that of St. Ignatius, her second bishop after St. Peter, from whom all our Patriarchs take their name, who suffered Martyrdom for the faith in A. D. 100?

Ignatius is familiarly called the "Child-like Saint," as it was generally believed by the early Christians that he was the child whom our Lord placed in the midst of the disputing disciples at Capernaum, and, holding him in His arms, said, "Except ye be converted and become as little children, ye shall not enter into the Kingdom of Heaven." Be this as it may, his after life is not out of keeping with that beautiful title. A saint he truly was, who laboured quietly for 40 or 50 years for his Master in Antioch, until at last, when quite an aged man, he was brought to Rome to suffer death. On his way to Rome he wrote his famous epistles at Smyrna. Continually in his Epistles these words occur: "Remember in your prayers the Church." These words I would pass on to you, for more, much more than in the days of Ignatius, does the Church of Antioch require your prayers. She has passed through persecution and massacre, war and pestilence, suffering severely not only from the neighbouring countries, who repeatedly fought upon her soil for supremacy, but also from the ambitions of other Christian communities. But the Church of Antioch did in the first three centuries contribute in no small degree to the building up of the Church universal. She fostered and nourished the Church in Palestine when the Hebrew Church of Jerusalem was scattered abroad. She took active part in the first three Councils, and helped to define and to maintain the Faith. From the days of the Patriarch Ignatius she furnished a noble array of witness for the truth, among them Eusebius, Mar Ephrem, Chrysostom, and many others, who are justly reckoned as Fathers of the Church. She witnessed with unshaken fidelity to the truth concerning the birth, life, death, resurrection and ascension of the Lord Jesus Christ. She treasured the written oracles of God and taught her people the Holy Scriptures as committed to their care by the Apostles. She preserved the constitution as delivered by them at Antioch to her, the first Church founded among the Gentles. And today what do we find? She is deprived of nearly all Christian and educational benefits, which we in England so happily possess. She exists among Mohammedan people and is dwelling in Mesopotamia. She needs our assistance, and she is asking us "To come over and help her."

These constitute Assyria's historical claims to recognition and justice. Strong as they are, her claims in more recent times are equally strong.

THREE: REASONS FOR EUROPEAN HELP

The sufferings of the Assyrian nation under Turkish misrule, and the agony she has undergone during the execution of the plan of extermination devised by the Turkish leaders, are equal to those of Armenia, although their existence has been far less widely realized. She has not merely shared Armenia's misfortunes, but on certain occasions her trials have been even more severe.

Our brave men have been tortured, killed, and massacred by thousands; our women have been taken into captivity and subjected to all sorts of abominable and unspeakable acts which cannot be stated here; our children by hundreds have been cut to pieces by the sword of the enemy as a pastime; our priests have been mocked, tortured, and murdered, and our homes plundered, and hundreds of our villages laid desolate. All these details have been mentioned as Armenian massacres, but Europe in general has not known the facts clearly. She has not known the facts clearly. She has not made any distinction between us and the Armenians, and therefore she has not taken special interest in, or expressed her sympathy with our nation and her cause. I was an eye-witness of the first massacre Diyarbakir, in which I lost three uncles, and only escaped myself in a miraculous manner two minutes before one of my uncles was killed. At the same time my father lost much of his fortune.

When the massacre began the Christians in the towns had some chance of defending themselves against the Turks, but the villagers were absolutely at the mercy of the Christians in the villages around Diyarbakir are Assyrians. This was especially true of the village of Keterbel, situated on the River Tigris, and all the Christians of the village were purely Assyrians, who, although outnumbered by ten to one, defended themselves for three days and nights, and were finally defeated when the assistance of regular Turkish troops from the town were secured. Posted on the walls of the town, they fired on the Assyrians, who, when hard pressed, took refuge in the church. When the Turks penetrated into the village every man, woman and child found there were killed immediately. The church, which was packed with refugees, was immediately surrounded. This edifice, a large, solidly built stone building, with an iron door and a domed roof, defied the attacks of the enemy for a while. Eventually they forced their way on to the roof, and having broken it open in the centre, a fire was lighted, and burning wood thrown down into the building. Before the devoted Assyrians could get door opened, half of the unfortunate occupants were burnt or suffocated, and the remainder were put to the sword without pity for age or sex.

This incident, which, alas, is only typical of what has been going on for the last 20 or 25 years, I mention because it came within my own experience. Nor are these atrocities horrible though they be, all that our unfortunate nation has been forced to endure. The cruelty of the Turks goes hand in hand with the grossest injustice, going back to an even earlier period than the first massacres. I will give two examples of this. For their truth I can vouch, since they occurred to the two members of my own family.

The first case is that of an estate belonging to my father, situated just outside my native town. As a boy I can well remember our possessing all the documents proving our ownership. The estate had been known by our name for centuries; but this did not prevent its confiscation. Despite all my father's efforts, the confiscation held good, and we were robbed without any chance of justice being obtained against the oppressor. The second case is that of one of my uncles (who eventually lost his life in the massacre referred to). He was a man of wealth and influence, and took over a copper mine from the Turkish Government. He worked this on his own account so successfully as to incur the jealousy of the Mohammedans, who procured an order and compelled him to cease work. Notwithstanding all his efforts – efforts which involved him in a great expenditure of time and money – he was denied justice, and his fortune, the greater part of which was sunk in the mine, was lost.

The Assyrians have done all that was humanly possible on their own initiative during the war. Assyrian troops, under the leadership of their patriarch, have performed prodigies of valour against overwhelming odds. By sheer weight of numbers they were driven back to Persia, after literally cutting their way through the Turkish forces. All this was done while labouring under the tremendous handicap of possessing no artillery.

Such have been the sufferings of the Assyrians, and such their achievements. An ancient nation, which has made immeasurable contributions to the knowledge of the world and to Christianity, has kept its separate existence alive despite the savage attacks of its enemies. It has done all that it could, and it appeals confidently to the justice of the Allies for its claims to be heard.

FOUR: ENGLAND AS THE MANDATORY POWER

Assyria is today greatly in the debt of Great Britain, France, and the United States for their missions, and the educational work they have already carried out. Neither does she forget the sympathy and appeals on her behalf made recently by the Archbishop of Canterbury, more especially on behalf of the Assyrian independent tribes on the Persian border. We remember with gratitude all that they have done for the spread of education and high ideals. I myself owe my first education to the American Mission for the Assyrians at Mardin, where I was a boarder for six years, and at which I obtained a diploma.

But more especially are we grateful for our recent part deliverance from the Turkish yoke. The news of the British occupation of southern Assyria has given us new courage, and our hearts go out in thankfulness to the gallant British force which has done so much in this distant land. The assistance afforded to Assyrian refugees who were driven by the Turks to the British lines from the N.W. Persian border will never be forgotten by us.

We ask: Is this chance of freedom to pass by? Are our sufferings and the oceans of blood which have been poured out to be of no avail? Northern Assyria is still in Turkish hands. Can anyone suggest that there is a solution possible except that which will, once and for all, free Assyria and Armenia, and guarantee both nations the same enjoyment of privileges and independence?

We venture that the new State should have her natural geographical boundaries and her separate existence, and be known by her own name – Assyria. We ask for the same treatment as will be meted out to Armenia and the Jews of Palestine, whether it be called autonomy or independence. We feel that the similarity of our sufferings with those of Armenia, the fight put up by our units, and our affinity to the Jews justify this request. Our chief object, nay, our only desire, is that Assyria should share the new life of these two nations under the mandatory of Great Britain. We hope that the principle of self determination and self administration will be adopted that we may have a chance to develop, and prove worthy of our claims to that independence which our nation has so rightly and so justly sought, and has proclaimed without hesitation.

The economic future of the country should be managed on the principles which President Wilson laid down. Whatever new schemes of irrigation or any other nature that may be undertaken, they should be conducted as though in an independent country, and for the benefit of the natives and of the State.

Some may say that the religious division of the people into Christians and Mohammedans militates against our claim. This is not true in our case; both sections are Assyrians, and were only kept apart by the intrigues of the Turks. There is no difference of language such as exists in Armenia. For instance, in the town of Mardin, in the province of Diyarbakir, where, as I mentioned before, I had my first education in the American college, the entire population and that of the surrounding districts both Christian and Mohammedan, is Assyrian by nationality. Very few Turks intermingle with them excepting the officials. If it were not for the instigation of the Turks, they would live together peaceably and amicably. I believe the case is the same all over Assyria. Left to our natural development the two halves will be welded into one, and this ancient race will once again exist as a sovereign people in those very lands which have been the scene of its great past.

Such are the facts I have to place before the British public. In these few words I have endeavoured to state the case of my country. I have touched upon her great and glorious past. I have mentioned a few of the horrors through which she has passed in more recent times. In my narrative of these I have confined myself to cases which have come under my own observation. Sad and dreadful as they are, they do not represent one hundredth part of that agony through which my nation has passed.

Yet, our hearts are filled with joy, and stirred with the high hopes of those ideals of justice and world-wide freedom which have been proclaimed, and for the realisation of which the Peace Conference now sits. These ideals which have been set before the world are the one and only sure hope of maintaining the blessings of civilization.

I state these facts not for myself, but on behalf of my nation, and, in her name, ask for that justice and independence to which the laws of nations entitle her.

We have passed through the fires of suffering, but we have ever held in mind what our past has been, and kept our eyes steadfastly fixed upon the goal before us. In confidence born of the impartiality of that tribunal before which we shall be heard, we state our case.

I have shown what we have done, and what we hope we shall be able to do. We realise that publicity will only benefit, and can never harm our cause; therefore we endeavour to bring it before as large a public as we possibly can. This is the claim that we have to put before the public, and we can with confidence leave them to judge for themselves.

INDEX

Suggestions for further reading

Aprim, Frederick A., *Assyrians: From Bedr Khan to Saddam Hussein. Driving into extinction the last Aramaic speakers* (2nd edition; Verdugo City, CA: Pearlida Publishing, 2007).

Bet-Sawoce, Jan, and Donef, Racho (eds.), *The struggle for a free Assyria: Documents on the Assyro-Chaldean delegation's political and diplomatic efforts, 1920–21* (Mesopotamian Series 3; Sydney: Tatavla Publishing, 2015).

Cetrez, Önver A., Donabed, Sargon George, and Makko, Aryo (eds.), *The Assyrian Heritage: Threads of continuity and influence* (Acta Universitatis Upsaliensis: Studies in Religion and Society 7; Uppsala; Uppsala University, 2012).

Dadesho, Sargon O., *The Assyrian national question at the United Nations: A historical injustice redressed* (Modesto, CA: Bet-Nahrain, 1987).

d'Bait Mar Shimun, Surma, *Assyrian church customs and the murder of Mar Shimun* (London: Faith Press, 1923).

de Courtois, Sébastien, *The forgotten genocide: eastern Christians, the last Arameans* (Piscataway, NJ: Gorgias Press, 2004).

Donabed, Sargon, *Remnants of heroes: the Assyrian experience: the continuity of the Assyrian heritage from Kharput to New England* (Chicago: Assyrian Academic Society Press, 2003).

Donabed, Sargon, and Donabed, Ninos, *Assyrians of Eastern Massachusetts* (Images of America; Charleston, SC: Arcadia, 2006).

Gaunt, David, *Massacres, resistance, protectors: Muslim-Christian relations in Eastern Anatolia during World War I* (Piscataway, NJ: Gorgias Press, 2006).

Gaunt, David, Atto, Naures, and Barthoma, Soner (eds.), *Let them not return: The genocide of the Assyrian, Syriac, and Chaldean Christians in the Ottoman Empire* (War and Genocide 26; New York, NY: Berghahn Books, 2017).

Haninke, Augin, *The Heirs of Patriarch Shaker* (Nineveh Press, forthcoming, 2017).

Lundgren, Svante, *The Assyrians: From Nineveh to Södertälje* (Raleigh, North Carolina: Nineveh Press, 2016).

Perley, David B., *A Collection of Writings on Assyrians* (Raleigh, North Carolina: Nineveh Press, 2016).

Shirinian, George, *Genocide in the Ottoman Empire: Armenians, Assyrians, and Greeks, 1913–1923* (New York, NY: Berghahn, 2017).

Travis, Hannibal, *Genocide in the Middle East: the Ottoman Empire, Iraq, and Sudan* (Durham, NC: Carolina Academic Press, 2010).

Travis, Hannibal (ed.), *The Assyrian genocide: Cultural and political legacies* (Routledge Studies in Modern History; forthcoming, 2017).

Yacoub, Joseph, *The Assyrian question* (2nd ed., Chicago: Alpha Graphic, 1993).

Yacoub, Joseph, *Year of the Sword: The Assyrian Christian genocide: A history* (London: C. Hurst & Publishers, 2016).

Tomas Beth-Avdalla is Project Manager for Modern Assyrian Research Archive (MARA).

Sargon George Donabed is Associate Professor of History and American Studies at Roger Williams University in Bristol, Rhode Island.

Modern Assyrian Research Archive (MARA) is a digital and physical archive founded by doctoral students and academic professionals interested in Assyrian Studies in 2008.

The aim of MARA is to locate, collect, and preserve source material and literature on the history, culture, and language of the Assyrian community from the 19th century onwards.

The source material digitized and made available by MARA comprises of digitized images of unpublished documents and manuscripts, non-copyrights publications, and audio recordings of oral sources collected from all over the world.

MARA's goal is to compile the world's largest digital and physical archive on Modern and Contemporary Assyrian culture by making use of extensive international private and professional networks.

Learn more about MARA by visiting www.assyrianarchive.org.

MARA COLLECTED TEXTS

1. Perley, David B; edited by Tomas Beth-Avdalla; foreword by Sargon George Donabed, *A Collection of Writings on Assyrians.* 734 pages, illustrations, index. ISBN 978-91-983441-0-3

2. Yoosuf, Abraham K.; edited by Tomas Beth-Avdalla; foreword by Sargon George Donabed, *Assyria and the Paris Peace Conference.* 246 pages, illustrations, index. ISBN 978-91-984100-1-3

Printed in Great Britain
by Amazon

79694168R00141